FROM SOLO TO SOULMATE

BREAK THE CYCLE.
ATTRACT THE ONE.
REWRITE YOUR LOVE STORY!

JOANNA HAIRABEDIAN

Pink Door
PUBLISHING

Disclaimer:
Neither the publisher nor the author is a medical doctor or licensed therapist. Nor are they engaged in rendering professional, medical advice, mental health or services to the reader.
The ideas, suggestions, recommendations of any kind, and activities provided in this book are not intended as a substitute for seeking professional or medical advice. Results are not guaranteed and depend on individual effort.
If you need professional help, seek a qualified healthcare provider or licensed counselor. This content is for educational purposes only and is not intended to treat, diagnose, or cure any diseases or issues. It is not a substitute for professional therapy advice, treatments or diagnosis. Some products or services mentioned may include affiliate links or partnerships, which means the author may receive a small commission or benefit at no additional cost to you. Only recommendations aligned with the author's values are shared.

Although the author and publisher have tried to ensure that the information in the book was correct at press time, they do not assume and hereby disclaim any liability to any party for any loss, damage, adverse effects, or disruption and ill-effects caused

Cover and Interior Layout @ 2025 Pink Door Marketing
Website: www.pinkdoormarketingagency.com
Email: tina@pinkdoormarketingagency.com

Ordering Information:

Special discounts are available on quantity purchases by groups, churches, and other associations. For details, please contact the author at the information provided at the back of this book.

2nd edition: From Solo to Soulmate (ISBN: 979-8-9938315-2-7)
1st edition: 7 Mistakes Women Make That Repel Good Men. (ISBN: 978-1-961641-11-2 Printed in The United States of America)

Dedication

To the beautiful women of all ages reading this book on the journey of love, inner transformation, and becoming the best version of you, the best is yet to come!

To the incredible man of my dreams, my husband, Dr. David Hairabedian. You are the wind underneath my wings and my number one supporter. Your love, support, wisdom, and insight help me birth this project!

To my wonderful besties, you know who you are in my family, prayer team, and friends for strengthening me with your love, support, prayers, and encouragement.

Acknowledgments

Teamwork makes the dream work! I want to thank the following people who played a part in helping me shape the book:

Tina Torres, the queen of marketing! You and the team from Pink Door Publishing did a fantastic job of getting the message out with this second edition of my book.

Lindi Stoler, the amazing book and media strategist! Your great book training and strategies for the first edition of this book helped bring my story to life. Without you, I wouldn't have the foundation stone for this book.

Carron Hairabedian, your sage wisdom and unending support was a source of energy to move me toward the finish line.

Terry Johnston, the years of business coaching, friendship and mentorship have inspired me to become a better version of myself, which influenced the birthing of my first book. Thank you for the awesome insights and co-creating Chapter 12 Decoding *His Dance Moves* in this second edition!

Dr. Lee Benton, for years as my TV Broadcast mentor and my powerful prayer warrior, you stood steadfast believing with me for the man of my dreams until he finally arrived.

Koren Emerson, you were one of the keys that helped unlock the love story for David and me.

Sharon Murphin, your honest feedback was invaluable. Your unwavering support, prayers and encouragement has been like the wind under my wings.

Zenobia Smith, my soul sister. Your watchful eye and protective heart during my courtship to David and now our marriage, has played a part in the love story we have today.

Liz Sheppard *(Bebe's & Liz's Clothing Boutique),* my amazing clothing stylist. You are truly the queen of fashion! Thank you for styling my beautiful look for the author's pic. You are the BEST!

Photo Credits

Kassel Row *(Kassel Photography)* **and Ralp Wood**, your photographic gifts beautifully immortalized my epic royal wedding. The picture of David and me in the Epilogue speaks a thousand words.

Daniel Pham Photography, thank you for the fabulous author/bio headshot.

Table of Contents

Dedication..i

Acknowledgement... ii

Contents..iv

Preface..vi

Introduction..ix

PART ONE: YOUR INNER TRANSFORMATION

Chapter One

The WIIFM Syndrome... 1

Chapter Two

Superhero Deactivators... 23

Chapter Three

The Beautiful You.. 39

Chapter Four

The Hidden Love Superpower.............................. 57

Chapter Five

The Kingmaker Vs. The Man-Breaker...................82

Chapter Six

The Reverse Trainer..98

Chapter Seven

The Disguised Doormat.......................................109

PART TWO: RELATIONAL DYNAMICS & DISCERNMENT

Chapter Eight

The Queen Of Chaos..128

Chapter Nine

The Director.. 145

Chapter Ten

The One-Upper…………………………………………………...…...162

Chapter Eleven

The Fantasizer…………………………………………………...........182

Chapter Twelve

Decoding His Dance Moves…………………………………….......…197

PART THREE: YOUR LOVE STORY REWRITTEN

Chapter Thirteen

Re-Writing Your Love Story…………………………….........…… 212

Chapter Fourteen

Defining Mr. Right!... 227

Epilogue

A Word From Joanna's Husband, Dr. David……………...….…… 259

About The Author………………………………....…..…..... 261

Appendix A…………………………...............…………….. 263

Appendix 1B & 2B……………………………….................…272

Preface

> *YOUR LOVE STORY ISN'T LATE. IT'S BEING WRITTEN*
> *WITH ETERNITY IN MIND.*
> ANONYMOUS

A Note from the Author

Are you ready for a fresh wind of hope, healing, and good change in your life? If so, you are in the right place at the right time.

Here's something that may greatly surprise you: nearly **70% of divorces are initiated by women — and in almost 30% of those cases, the men had no idea their wives were that unhappy.**

Let that sink in.

Whether you're a businesswoman, influencer, single mom, or a woman who's been single too long, feels stuck in your current relationship or tired of surviving on love breadcrumbs, we all share one deep desire: **to be seen, heard, and understood by the man we love.**

At the heart of many broken relationships is not a lack of love — but unmet expectations, communication breakdowns, and the quiet ache of feeling invisible.

So what causes women to walk away?

More often than not, it's this: **they no longer feel seen, heard, or emotionally connected with their man.**

Many women were never taught how to heal the relationship patterns, emotional wounds, and inner triggers that quietly sabotage love from the inside out.

Research shows that relationships often fall apart for simple reasons: people don't communicate well, react emotionally, carry unhealed trauma, or never learned how to resolve conflict in a healthy, loving way.

The unhealed patterns repeat. You end up with a different man. You experience the same pain or the same rejection and loneliness.

It becomes the wash-rinse-repeat cycle of hurt and disappointment.

If you've ever whispered, *"Is there really someone out there for me?"* you're not alone. Many women who are capable, strong and successful, feel this same ache!

Let's get real—aren't there days when dating feels like searching for a parking spot at the grocery store? All the good ones are taken, and the rest are… not exactly what you prayed for. I understand. Been there, done that.

Maybe you're wondering if God has overlooked you? He hasn't. It's not too late — and there is hope for you!

Here's the truth your heart needs to hear: **If it happened for me, it could absolutely happen for you!** Healthy, emotionally intelligent, and spiritual men *do* exist.

The key is becoming aligned, healed, and emotionally open to attracting the healthy kind of love you desire and deserve.

I'm a Relationship Coach and Soulmate Strategist and I help women rewrite their love stories from the inside out.

This book is your soul-transforming guide that will help increase your skills to be heard and seen in a healthy relationship.

It serves as a powerful, gentle truth mirror and a compassionate compass that reveals the damaging relationship patterns you've unknowingly repeated.

Inside these pages, we'll laugh together, reflect and get real about love. You'll learn how to attract a God-aligned love, improve your communication skills, strengthen your emotional intelligence, and protect your marriage from the patterns that sabotage so many relationships today.

By the final page, you'll know how to identify and recognize the right man when God brings him into your life. You'll know how to build a relationship that honors Him and celebrates your worth.

So, beautiful one, are you ready to break old cycles, invite in the right one, and rewrite your love story?

If your heart says *yes*, then grab your favorite coffee or tea, settle in, and let's begin this sacred, life-changing journey together.

Let's rewrite your love story.

With heartfelt sincerity,

Joanna Hairabedian

Introduction

> *THERE ARE EASIER THINGS IN LIFE THAN TRYING*
> *TO FIND A NICE GUY, LIKE*
> *NAILING AN OUNCE OF JELLY TO A TREE.*
> ANONYMOUS

It's a funny quote, but doesn't it feel so true sometimes? Especially if you've ever felt the sting of loneliness while watching other couples in love.

Have you ever wondered why love seems so easy for everyone else… but so complicated for you? Have you ever found yourself lying awake at night asking God, *"Why hasn't it happened for me yet?"*

Maybe you've asked yourself:
"What does she have that I don't have?"
"Where are all the good guys?"
"Will I finally have a valentine this year?"

If so, you're not alone! In fact, you're in the exact place where transformation begins.

The truth is, there are behaviors that **attract** a great guy and behaviors that **repel** him. Every woman has operated in at least one of the behaviors that unknowingly push good men away, whether she meant to or not.

I spent years wrestling with unanswered prayers, disappointments and romantic missteps that left me wondering if a loving partnership was even possible.

And to make it worse, I could hear my biological clock ticking louder with each passing year, all while fielding the relentless, well-meaning questions:

"Why don't you have a boyfriend yet?"
"Are you being too picky?"
"Have you tried online dating?"

Did I eventually meet and marry Mr. Right — my incredible soulmate — and experience my God-written happily-ever-after?

Absolutely. Beautifully so.

But before we get to the happily-ever-after, we need to start at the real beginning.

The truth is… sometimes our man-picker is broken. Mine sure was.

In my younger years, I met and fell in love with an ex (whom I'll call *"Mr. Wrong"*). Mr. Wrong may sound cliché, but for the sake of teaching, I'm going to use a few labels throughout this book: Mr. Wrong, Mr. Potential, and Mr. Right. You'll see why.

Back then, I believed in fairy tales. Like so many women, I dreamed of love and partnership. I truly thought that my knight would sweep me off my feet and rescue me from life's trials.

Together we'd build a beautiful life filled with adventure, romance, and happily-ever-after-endings. But reality didn't match the dream.

On the second day of my first marriage, my new husband—Mr. Wrong—the man I believed was my forever, looked at me with stone-cold eyes and said,
"I don't love you."

The silence that followed was deafening. I felt the blood drain from my face. I stood there, stunned, as if the floor had vanished beneath my feet.

"WHY did you pressure me to get married? Wha, wha, whyyyy didn't you talk to me when I asked what was wrong?" I stammered, my voice cracking.

With a blank stare, he answered flatly, *"When I talked to our friends about it, they said it was probably just fear."*

Everyone else knew...but ME.

The Slow Unraveling

Over the months that followed, the painful truth began to unfold.

Behind the charming exterior was a man secretly wrestling with a well-hidden alcohol addiction. He was controlling, had a casual relationship with the truth, and an inability to love faithfully.

Was he like this while we were dating? Noooo. He was wonderful. Quick with a joke and full of laughter and a great dancer.

I never once saw him have more than a single drink. He ministered to the youth in church, shared his testimony, and spoke of God's goodness. Everyone I knew believed he'd make a great husband.

And so, I stayed. I prayed. I fought for our marriage. I clung to the belief that behind every addiction is an aching heart in need of love. I told myself that my love could heal him, could change him.

We separated three times over two years, each time by my decision, desperate to establish healthy boundaries. Yet sadly, each time, I returned, holding onto his promises to change.

But the patterns never stopped. He continued with the isolation tactics, the gaslighting, the motional coldness, rejection, betrayal and shattered dreams.

He didn't want me, yet he wouldn't let me go.

Worse still, fear began creeping into the corners of my nights. I'd wake up to find the front door wide open—Mr. Wrong gone, vanished into the darkness. There was no explanation of where he went or why. Yep, I could pick 'em!

And then, one day, the hair on the back of my neck stood up as I uncovered secret emails from his lover. Attached were articles about a man who had murdered his wife to collect the insurance and then returned to his ex-girlfriend.

In that moment, terror gripped my soul. I cried out in desperate prayer:

"God, what do I do? If this isn't going to get better… make a way to get me out!"

The Power of Prayer and the Way of Escape

An unexpected way of escape presented itself just two weeks after that desperate prayer.

It happened during dinner at a restaurant when I had suggested going to a Christian music event after we were done eating. Without warning, he exploded:

"If you're going to desecrate our marriage like that, you can pack your bags and GET OUT!"

What he didn't know was that this time… I was ready!

Quietly, over the previous months, I had been preparing a way of escape. I rented a room and opened a private savings account. I made a plan to leave with my dignity and my safety intact.

On that night, I did.

I packed my things, loaded what I could fit into the car, and drove away. No one helped me. No one carried my bags. I left and never looked back.

Prayer steadied my trembling hands as I closed that chapter of my life. And faith kept my heart beating when fear threatened to silence it.

A New Beginning, But Not Overnight

Even after leaving, the road to healing wasn't immediate. Harassment followed. Threats lingered like shadows. Fear and intimidation crept into the quiet spaces of my days and nights.

Concerned for my safety, some friends who lived in Europe invited me to visit. A move that proved to be both a physical rescue and a spiritual reawakening. I left the U.S. with nothing but two carry-on bags and a heart in pieces.

It was there, on a cold, rainy night in Europe, lying broken in the middle of an *"ugly cry moment"* on the kitchen floor of an apartment, that I cried out:

"God, show me how I ended up in this disaster! My life is shattered! Hold up a spiritual mirror to my face and show me what I need to see about myself."

And He did.

What I saw wasn't easy. But that sacred moment of surrender, filled with courage, honesty, and raw vulnerability, marked the true beginning of my transformation.

It takes courage to lean in, to face the good, the bad, and the ugly about yourself, and to choose to forgive and accept yourself anyway. If I could do it, you could too!

Walking into the unknown of change requires courage. It's a decision to say *"No"* to fear and *"Yes"* to courage, and to take the steps it takes to live differently.

And you can do this!

Road Back to Hope

Healing wasn't linear. Some days, I stood tall, reclaiming my independence, my strength, and my sense of self. My career was thriving. My friends were wonderful.

But other days, the waves of loneliness and jealousy would bite as I watched others build the kind of lives I had once dreamed of for myself.

As time went on, the unexpected happened: the clock kept ticking. Year after year, I was still a divorcée. Five years. Eight years. Eleven years. Still single. Still waiting. Still daring to hope.

But through it all, one truth anchored me: God wasn't done writing my story yet. He's not done writing yours either.

Over time, after much frustration, reflection, and tears, I realized something crucial. I had to understand how I attracted and married a man like Mr. Wrong, someone who was the exact opposite of what I truly desired. Then, I had to evaluate why I allowed myself to be pressured into a marriage I wasn't at peace with.

And finally, this one stung, I had to accept responsibility for my own part of mistakes in the marriage, regardless of his behavior.

This book will delve into every aspect of this.

> *YOU ARE ACCOUNTABLE FOR YOUR ACTIONS,*
> *YOUR DECISIONS, YOUR LIFE;*
> *NO ONE ELSE BUT YOU.*
> CATHERINE PULSIFER, YOUR POSITIVE OASIS

On my journey of inner transformation, I uncovered powerful lessons that can help you avoid marrying your own Mr. Wrong. They can also shorten your learning curve, helping you attract and keep your Mr. Right—or deepen the relationship you're already in.

Understanding is the Beginning of Knowledge

Identifying my part in the failure of the marriage didn't excuse Mr. Wrong's bad behavior, not for a moment. But I had to be willing to look at my side of the coin, in addition to healing from the hurts he caused.

As my journey of healing and transformation progressed, I began to realize several key things:

My words, my attitudes, my hidden mindsets, and my unspoken fears were subtly repelling the very love I longed for. They were quietly keeping me stuck inside the singles' circle.

I call them **Superhero Deactivators**, subconscious patterns and behaviors that deactivate a good man's natural instincts to pursue, protect, and cherish. We'll dive deeper into this later in the book.

Once I learned to recognize and transform the superhero deactivators, everything began to shift.

As my awareness and emotional intelligence grew, I noticed how many other amazing women were unknowingly operating in the very same patterns I once did.

Meeting Mr. Right

Each individual journey is different, but one truth I've learned is this: before we're truly ready for Mr. Right, it's essential to heal from past trauma and heartbreak.

I had walked through a long season of healing and personal transformation before I met my husband, Dr. David. When we crossed paths, I was in a great heart space, healed, and confident in my identity. I wasn't searching for or chasing love. **But love found me when I was finally ready to receive it.** The same can happen for you.

We were introduced casually by a mutual friend, not for romance, but for a potential business collaboration. At the time, David lived in Missouri, and I was in California. There were no immediate fireworks. No storybook swirl. Just mutual respect. Friendship. Spiritual alignment.

We became friends and prayer partners first. Neither of us was initially attracted to each other. But over time, we began to grow together, to trust, and to build a foundation rooted in faith, friendship, and purpose.

We worked on various projects together, prayed through life's challenges, and I quietly observed how he responded and carried himself in various situations.

Little keys unlock big doors, and big doors swing on small hinges.

And then one day, the spark ignited. It was undeniable. It was as if God pulled a veil from both of our eyes, and in that moment, we saw what had been growing between us all along. Instant chemistry. And it felt right.

Today, more than a decade later, we're traveling the world together, laughing together, building a love story rooted in faith, friendship, and unwavering devotion.

What It Means for You

If it could happen to me, it could happen to you!

And it begins right here, with awareness. With a little courage. If we aren't aware of what needs to change, how can we make changes for the better?

Imagine the day you stop striving for love and start becoming the kind of woman who naturally attracts it. Imagine feeling cherished, chosen, and celebrated, simply because you aligned your heart with heaven's best for you.

This journey isn't about desperation. It's about preparation. It's about becoming.

And what's the first key you hold? It's the one we'll uncover in the next chapter called, **The WIIFM Syndrome:** *What's In It For Me?*

This key opens doors of insight most women have never realized are silently souring good relationships or sabotaging the very love they long for.

And yes, it's something our culture and media have unknowingly helped perpetuate.

Ready to see yourself, and love, in a whole new light?

Let's get started!

Chapter One

THE WIIFM SYNDROME
(What's In It For Me?)

> ***I'M NOT SELFISH. I JUST KNOW THAT THE WORLD***
> ***REVOLVES AROUND ME.***
> ANONYMOUS

All joking aside, it seems like today's world has perfected the art of self-centeredness and there are:

- More takers than givers.
- More talkers than listeners.
- People who expect you to fix their problems… yet disappear the moment you need support.
- Relationships built on what someone can *get*, instead of what they're willing to *give*.

And if we're completely honest?

Sometimes we're not just the victims — we've been the participants too.

Remember, there are two sides to every coin. One side of the coin are the women; the other side of the coin are the men. In this book, we are looking at our side of the coin as women.

This subtle self-focus is what I call, **The WIIFM Syndrome**. *"What's In It For Me?" It* is one of the keys that can sabotage love in a relationship.

It starts small, doesn't it? It can be a motive, a wish or a thought: *"What can he do for me?"*

It sounds innocent enough. But if left unchecked, it quietly builds an invisible wall around the heart, a wall good men can't climb.

Before we unpack the bigger relationship saboteurs later in this book, we need to start with three core topics introduced in these first three chapters.

These foundational truths shape everything that follows and are essential for building healthy, lasting relationship dynamics.

The first foundation stone is what I call **The WIIFM Syndrome**.

And as I've said before, it takes courage and humility to examine ourselves honestly—to look at the beautiful parts of who we are, as well as the parts that may need healing or growth.

CONGRATULATIONS! You're doing it.

That already sets you apart from *most* women.

You're doing the brave inner work many women avoid. And now that you're here, it's time to look at the deeper attitudes and subtle mindsets that quietly shape how we show up in love.

> *WHEN LOVE BECOMES A TRANSACTION, WE STOP*
> *SEEING HEARTS.*
> ANONYMOUS

This is a poignant quote, and it's so important to recognize when a relationship is **transactional** versus **relational**.

Let's take a look at how this relates to the WIIFM Syndrome.

The Two Faces of *"What's In It For Me?"*

There's a healthy WIIFM:

You know your worth, value, and setting and maintaining healthy boundaries. It's relational and involves mutual respect. The heart's focus is on serving others as well as receiving love and care in return.

It's about healthy reciprocity, equal give and equal take. These are the qualities that help us do good business and have great relationships.

But there's also an unhealthy WIIFM:

Selfishness, constant complaining, entitlement *("You owe me")*, or a victim mentality *("I can't because...")*. It's transactional. The heart's focus is all about yourself and a running list of reasons why you can't or won't move forward.

It expects someone else to rescue you, often placing misplaced reliance on a man to fill voids that only God and personal growth can truly address.

It's a one-sided, self-focused mindset, where you position yourself as the primary receiver without truly offering your best in return. Being real and vulnerable, these inner motivations played a part in why I married Mr. Wrong.

I also think it's important we acknowledge how this **WIIFM Syndrome** has been on the rise. Our culture today often cultivates a self-absorbed, sometimes narcissistic, and frequently victim-centered mentality. We don't take responsibility; we blame others. I know I did.

At first, I blamed God. I blamed Mr. Wrong. I blamed the people who abandoned me. I blamed the friends who betrayed me.

I blamed the world for the pain I felt over marrying the wrong man.

It was all about my pain, my feelings, and my victimhood.

Yes, I needed to heal. But healing couldn't begin until I left my pity party.

One of my life coaches once made a profound statement. She said, *"Joanna, I give myself permission to change my mind when given new information. I encourage you to do the same."*

It's so easy to get stuck in an old mindset, one that's no longer serving you or bringing the results you desire in life. I took her advice to heart, and let me tell you, it was a game changer.

Let's pause for a moment right here.

Go ahead, place your hand over your heart and say out loud:

"I give myself permission and grace to change my mind when I receive new information."

Way to go, beautiful!

I had to evaluate my actions and choices with Mr. Wrong. I had to ask myself why I allowed someone to pressure me into marriage. And then, I had to accept responsibility for my mistakes within that marriage, regardless of his behavior.

Understanding my part in the failure of the marriage didn't excuse his actions. It empowered me to take ownership of my choices, learn from them, and become a stronger, wiser version of myself.

It would have been easy, so easy to play the victim. To blame Mr. Wrong for every bad thing he did and never stop to understand how I wound up in a marriage that felt like it was forged in hell.

But if I hadn't been willing to learn from those mistakes, I would have kept spinning in the same wash, rinse, repeat cycle, headed for a second, third, or even fourth divorce.

Ready to go deeper?

If so, I've got you. Let's do this!

Most of the time, we don't realize just how much selfishness quietly influences our choices. It certainly did for me, and it led me down some painfully difficult roads.

I wish I'd paid attention to this timeless quote many consider the gold standard for examining ourselves!

> *LOVE IS PATIENT. LOVE IS KIND. IT DOES NOT ENVY, IT DOES NOT BOAST, IT IS NOT PROUD. IT DOES NOT DISHONOR OTHERS, IT IS NOT SELF-SEEKING, IT IS NOT EASILY ANGERED, IT KEEPS NO RECORD OF WRONGS. LOVE DOES NOT DELIGHT IN EVIL BUT REJOICES WITH THE TRUTH. IT ALWAYS PROTECTS, ALWAYS TRUSTS, ALWAYS HOPES, ALWAYS PERSEVERES.*
> 1 CORINTHIANS 13:4-7, NIV

Now that we've uncovered and understand the foundations of **The WIIFM Syndrome** and its impact on our relationships, it's time to delve deeper.

Let's shine a light on social predictive media programming, the subtle (and not-so-subtle) messages that quietly shape how we see ourselves and others.

These cultural cues don't just influence our preferences; they can distort our God-given identity and reroute the path to healthy love.

Believe it or not, it all starts with something as simple as a doll.

My Ken and Barbie Lessons

When I was growing up, I loved to play with my Barbie and Ken dolls. The stories I created were in part influenced by Disney movies and shows I used to watch.

As little girls, we absorb media messages early, and often without even realizing it. For example, my Barbie world taught me several things:

- Good Barbie likes Ken, and Ken likes her.
- Jealous, bad Barbie tries to steal Ken from good Barbie.
- Bad Barbie does something cruel to get good Barbie out of the way.
- Ken rescues good Barbie.
- Good Barbie wins and lives happily ever after with Ken.

The lessons were clear, and problematic:

- Women steal other women's men.
- A man will come to your rescue.
- A man will complete you.

But what Barbie never taught me was this: **healing your own heart is the real fairytale.**

And it's one you can write for yourself.

The seeds of WIIFM thinking don't just come from childhood games. They're constantly reinforced by media stereotypes that subtly shape how we view love, men, women, and marriage.

Let me ask you something.

How often do we see TV shows or movies that teach women how to grow into their true identity as royalty, from the inside out? Where are the stories that empower girls to value themselves, to honor their bodies, and to walk in grace, strength, and self-respect?

Now, contrast that with what so many of our young women and girls are exposed to today: music videos and lyrics that condition them to use sex as a tool for control and manipulation. Songs that glamorize promiscuity, prostitution, and normalize women being objectified with their perceived value coming from being sexualized.

Even something as seemingly innocent as social media filters, slimming faces, plumping lips, and adding flirty eyes, can subtly teach girls that their natural, God-given beauty isn't enough.

It's also called **subtle grooming.**

Let's talk about a form of grooming that often goes unnoticed, not in dark alleyways or behind locked doors, but on bright stages and inside everyday culture.

I had a wake-up call at a dance competition for a friend's daughter.

The stage was filled with sweet little girls, but what they were wearing caught me off guard: heavy *"big girl"* makeup, tight-fitting, grown-woman costumes, and dance routines choreographed to lyrics that were anything but age-appropriate.

It wasn't overtly sinister, but it was subtle, seductive in its normalization. Then later, I saw Facebook posts of these same little girls posing in *"grown woman"* stances, sticking out their booties and making sultry faces for the camera.

Do you see what's happening here?

It's subtle.

This is grooming in disguise when innocence is dressed up in sensuality and sold as *"cute"* or *"entertainment"*.

These seemingly small exposures add up, quietly shaping how our daughters begin to see themselves, their bodies, and their worth.

And what about our boys? What are they being groomed for?

Far too often, they're being influenced by music, videos, and social media that degrade women, reducing them to *"hoes"* and *"bitches"*. Instead of learning to honor, protect, and cherish women, they're being conditioned to dominate, disrespect, use for sex, and discard them like yesterday's news.

Then there's the world of video games, where rewards often come through aggression, violence, and domination, teaching boys that power equals masculinity, while emotion, respect, and restraint are signs of weakness.

And don't even get me started on unchecked exposure to pornography. It blurs their ability to see women as sacred, valuable equals created in the image of God. It turns connection into consumption.

> *THE MASS MEDIA... TEACHES US NOT TO TRUST*
> *REAL INTIMACY, BUT*
> *TO CRAVE ATTENTION.*
> BELL HOOKS

All of this messaging lays the groundwork for unhealthy relationships, disrespectful attitudes, and distorted views of love. Sadly, most of the time we don't even realize how deeply this conditioning shapes us, until one day, we wake up and wonder:

"Why does love feel so broken?"

"Why am I on my third marriage?"

Think about how often we come across magazine articles and online posts about *"getting the man"*. So many of them focus on how to get him to buy you things or how to use sex as a bargaining chip to get what you want.

Whether it's videos, movies, lyrics, social media, or clickbait headlines, the underlying soundbite is the same:

"What can you do for me, and what do I have to give up or take to get it?"

It's thought-provoking, isn't it?

On the following page, you'll find a table listing some of the most common media stereotypes about men and women. As you read through them, I invite you to pause and reflect on a few important questions:

- Do you see your identity connected to any of the media programming or stereotypes?
- Are any of your perspectives about men or yourself identifiable with some of these stereotypes?
- What part of these mindsets played a part in your relationship's failure because of unrealistic or unmet expectations?
- Have any of these stereotypes made you feel pressured to conform or change yourself to attract or keep a man?
- Are there areas where media, entertainment, or peer culture have influenced you more than you'd like to admit?
- And lastly, what *"Barbie lessons"* did you learn growing up, and how does that play into media stereotype you have been exposed to?

Reflection...

Take a moment to think about some key experiences in your life that were shaped by media messaging and how those influences may have impacted your choices in love and life.

It's a lot like the old story of the lobster being cooked slowly, unaware the water is heating up until it's too late.

Over time, we can unknowingly start equating passion with unpredictability, chemistry with chaos, and self-worth with someone else's validation.

The **WIIFM** mindset *(What's In It For Me?)* is constantly, subtly reinforced through influencers, social media, and on-screen fantasies.

It teaches us to prioritize image over intimacy, to chase likes instead of connection and to swipe left or right on the dating app.

And what about the culture we see in certain corners of Hollywood, where some women boast about using men and refer to them as *"pay pigs"?*

The game isn't about building true connections or earning mutual respect, it's about what they can get him to buy.

But here's the truth: Real love doesn't come with a filter.

Love comes with character. It comes with commitment.

It comes with the courage to grow beyond the scripts we've inherited.

The media does an exceptional job of creating stereotypes about both men and women, and whether we realize it or not, those portrayals can deeply impact our behaviors, beliefs, and choices, not just in how we treat others, but in how we see and value ourselves.

Let's take a closer look at some of them.

Common Media Stereotypes of Men and Women

Stereotype of a Man	Stereotype of a Woman
The Fairytale Prince	**The Fairytale Princess**
(Perfect rescuer riding in on a white horse)	(Perfect beauty waiting to be saved)
The Bumbling Husband	**The Damsel in Distress**
(Clueless, inept, dominated by the wife)	(Helpless, always needing rescue)
The "Bad Boy" Alpha Male	**The Seductress**
(Ultra-dominant, sexy, controlling)	(Uses beauty to manipulate men)
The Nice Guy	**The Nagging Wife/Girlfriend**
(Passive, finishes last, never gets the girl)	(Critical, hard to please, emasculating)
The Pushover	**The Career-Obsessed Woman**
(Weak, easily controlled)	(Cold, heartless, ruthless)
The Business Tycoon	**The Weak Woman**
(Narcissistic, seductive, power-hungry)	(Overly emotional, needy, irrational)

Think about the damaging relationship messages media programming sends to us:

- Women are taught to use beauty, sex, or manipulation instead of wisdom and character.

- Men are taught to either dominate… or become passive doormats.
- Both men and women are programmed to be transactional, not relational, to focus on *"getting what you can."*
- Romance is depicted as conquest, control, usury, or rescue, rarely as healthy, equal partnership.

No wonder healthy, wonderful love can feel so out of reach when we've been programmed to believe we must:

- Seduce to be valued.
- Be rescued to be worthy.
- Win over someone's heart through control, performance, or people-pleasing.
- Use sex to get material things. The "things" that won't hold your hand when you're sick or speak life into you when your heart is broken.

It's no surprise relationships collapse under the crushing weight of toxic, unrealistic expectations.

When I married Mr. Wrong, I was still carrying my hidden **WIIFM** hopes:

- He'll rescue me.
- He'll fulfill my dreams.
- He'll meet all my needs.
- He'll take care of me financially.

But instead, reality hit like a punch to the gut.

"I don't love you," he said, two days after our wedding.

In hindsight, those unmet needs and unfulfilled dreams were never his to carry. I had handed him a role he was never meant to fill.

Sidebar: When Good Men Go Unseen

More to come on this in the next chapter. During my research interviews for the book, I sat with several good men, thoughtful, respectful, emotionally available. The kind many women say they want.

And yet, they echoed similar, eerie stories. *"I'm **too** nice."* Or *"She rejected my kindness as weakness".* (My husband David can also attest to his experiences of being told he's too nice.)

One was 45 years, successful, kind-hearted, and single. *"I treat women well,"* he said, *"but it's like they're bored. They want the "bad boy", not me. So, I'm rejected."*

Another, just 23 years, shared something that stopped me cold. He said, *"I'm dating a guy now because it's drama-free. I prefer women, but with them it's always criticism, rejection and chaos. I'd rather be with someone who accepts me and not try to change me and NO drama."*

Let that sink in.

Now, are women responsible for a man's romantic choices? No, of course not. But do we influence them? Profoundly. *(Remember the Hollywood women who discard men like dirty napkins with the name "pay pigs. ")*

Do you see it? The media's seductive whisper, threading through movie plots, pop songs, and sitcoms: *Bad boys are exciting. Good men are boring. Chase the danger. Lust. Tame the beast.*

And then we wonder why our hearts are broken again and again.

In the quiet space between those interviews, I realized something sobering: many women don't just miss the good men, they can unintentionally damage them. Criticism in the name of *"helping."* Rejection in the name of *"chemistry."* Dismissal disguised as *"just being honest."*

They often pass over kindness for chemistry, respect for edge, and then wonder why their hearts are like a broken record that spins over and over.

The media has trained us to crave intensity over intimacy. But real connection, the kind that lasts, is often found in the gentle steadiness of a good man.

We'll explore more in the next chapter on the ways women can damage good men. But for now, consider - Have you overlooked a good man? What kind of man have you been drawn to… and why?
And more importantly… How have you made the good ones feel?

My Gym Date Revelation

Later, during my single years, a handsome man from my gym invited me to dinner.

We had a great connection, easy conversation, good banter, and what felt like instant chemistry.

The date was everything I'd hoped for, until I talked and talked…and talked.

He made me feel so comfortable, like I could share anything, so I did. I shared my opinions, my many complaints, my frustrations about this and that. Meanwhile, Mr. Potential barely got a word in.

That turned out to be **my** one and only date with Mr. Potential.

I felt rejected and couldn't figure out why he wasn't interested in going out again. We seemed to have such a great connection.

In a big courage moment, sweat practically dripping down my back, I asked him why he'd cooled off. And with kind, gentle honesty, he said:

"Joanna, you're a great person… but it's all about you. And all you did was complain about everything."

OUCH!

And yet, that truth-telling moment was a gift, a mirror, and it changed me forever.

As embarrassing as it was to hear, it forced me to stop and really consider what he said. Essentially, I'd ignored him. I hadn't cared to know about him, and I was entirely absorbed in myself.

Can you say **WIIFM?**

To this day, I'm thankful he had the courage to tell me the truth. And I'm grateful I had the maturity to receive it, reflect on it, and recognize what needed to change and heal in me.

From that moment on, I decided:

Anyone who spends time with me will leave feeling blessed, heard, and encouraged in some way.

I would learn to use my two ears to listen more and my one mouth to speak less.

Annette, Joshua, and the Dinner that Wasn't

A former associate, Annette, had been single for quite a while and was eager to *"find a man."* I thought my friend Joshua might be a good match for her, so I invited Annette to join us for dinner.

Joshua was smart, kind, successful, and attractive. Plus, both of them were foodies, it seemed like a natural fit.

But during dinner, the unexpected happened.

Annette dominated the entire evening. She interrupted him repeatedly, talked over him, and eagerly showcased her vast knowledge about everything under the sun.

It was all about her.

Not once did she pause to ask about him, his interests, his experiences, his story. It was eye-opening to witness firsthand.

At the end of the night, she even asked him out. Joshua, ever the gentleman, politely declined.

And that's when the real issue surfaced.

Annette was upset, hurt, and felt rejected. But instead of pausing to reflect, she blamed him. She couldn't understand why he didn't want to go out with her.

Another opportunity was lost, not because she wasn't wonderful, talented, or attractive, but because her **WIIFM** self-focus repelled him.

Bonus Romance Tip: Guys need an opening to invite you on a date.

Allow Mr. Potential the opportunity to ask you out and take the lead.

You can do this by dropping subtle hints or casual suggestions that make it easy for him to invite you to a date. For example, if you're both foodies, you might say, *"I've heard about this new restaurant that's supposed to be amazing. I've been meaning to try it."* Or if you're into sports, you could mention, *"I love going to live games, the energy is so fun!"*

This gives him a sense of direction and helps reduce his fear of rejection. And if he's genuinely interested, he'll ask you out.

Choosing a Different Response Leads to a Different Result

WIIFM *(What's In It For Me?)* is sneaky, and it's everywhere.

It shows up when we interrupt instead of listen, talk over instead of lean in, or expect instead of honor. And it quietly suffocates the very connection we long to experience.

Here are four powerful lessons I learned from my own journey, and from those around me:

Lesson 1: Dealing with the Selfish Mindset

Shift from *"What can he do for me?"* to *"How can we serve each other's purpose and joy?"*

Ask yourself: How can I honor what matters to this person, especially Mr. Potential?

Lesson 2: Seeing Beyond Stereotypes

Stop measuring men against fantasy standards shaped by movies, magazines, or social media. See them for who they really are.

Be curious. Ask questions. Seek to understand their hopes, their dreams, their fears. Seek out "the nice guy."

Lesson 3: Listening with Both Ears and One Heart

Give people the gift of your presence.

Ask thoughtful questions.

Listen deeply.

Value others without an agenda or motive.

Listen more than you speak.

Lesson 4: Taking Radical Ownership

Refrain from constant complaining and blaming.

Own your healing. Own your journey.

Own your happiness before you ask someone else to build a life with you.

Now imagine this...

Entering a love relationship where you're already whole, radiant, and free. You're not desperate for rescue. You're not demanding perfection, but simply open, with an ability to receive, and soft enough to give.

This is the kind of love story heaven has always had in mind for you.

Great job, beautiful. Ready to get this party started?

In the next chapter, we'll uncover behavior patterns that unknowingly deactivate and damage a good man's inner superhero, often without us even realizing it.

We'll also explore the man mirror, the reflection you're holding up to the men who cross your path.

But before we turn onto the next chapter, let's pause.

Take a moment to go through the practical application and journal meditations. These exercises are a crucial step in retraining your behaviors.

Reflection Prayer...

Lord, open my eyes to where fear or fantasy have shaped my view of love. Heal my heart from the subtle lies that have taught me to take instead of serve. Teach me to see myself and others through Your eyes. Prepare my heart to love deeply, honor fully, and build beautifully. Amen.

Journal Meditations

- What media stereotypes about love have I unknowingly believed or engaged in?
- In what areas of my life have I operated with a *"What's In It for Me?"* mindset?
- How would my relationships shift if I loved from a place of abundance instead of need?

Practical Application Challenge

This week, invite someone, a friend, coworker, or even a new acquaintance, out for lunch or coffee.

- Make it your intention to support them and listen intently to what they share.
- Ask them to share an experience that was life-changing or deeply meaningful for them.
- As they speak, resist the urge to give your opinion or talk about yourself.
- Simply listen. Affirm. Validate. Honor their story.

Notice how they respond to being seen and heard. Pay attention to their facial expressions, body language, and energy.

Then, conclude the lunch by offering them a kind affirmation, maybe a word of encouragement, a blessing, or a short prayer.

Your goal is simple:

To make them feel blessed, seen, and heard.

The purpose of the exercise is to create an awareness of how to make your man feel heard and blessed.

Date of the lunch: _____

Journal Your Lunch Experience Below, Reflecting on the Following:

- How many times did you feel the urge to interrupt or shift the conversation?
- What was their story? What stood out to you?
- How did it feel to sit quietly, listen deeply, and fully focus on them while they were sharing?
- Did your mind wander? If so, what brought it back?
- How do you think they felt after this encounter with you?
- Was there anything else you noticed, about them or about yourself?

_____

_____

_____

_____

_____

_____

_____

_____

_____

_____

_____

_____

_____

_____

_____

_____

_____

_____

_____

_____

_____

_____

_____

_____

_____

_____

_____

_____

_____

You're doing great!!

You're showing such beautiful courage and humility, and this is just the beginning.

You're stepping into a whole new world, and I couldn't be more excited for you.

Heart Reflections ✒
FROM JOANNA

Way to go, cherished one!

You're stepping into the courageous journey of becoming a **Kingmaker**, and I'm so proud of the inner work you're doing.

Take a moment to pause and breathe. How did this chapter make you feel? What stood out the most?

If you need a break—grab a drink, take a walk, or put on uplifting music—then come back refreshed and ready for more.

Celebrate every moment of clarity, even the ones that sting.
Those "ouch" moments are where real change begins. Acknowledge what surfaced, accept it with grace, and be encouraged: you now have the power to choose differently.

You're entering a new season of renewed mindset, fresh heart posture, and a higher frequency radiating from within you.

Okay, beautiful… ready for the next key?

In the next chapter, we'll uncover **Superhero Deactivators**—subtle behaviors that can unintentionally repel a good man or erode connection.

Your next breakthrough is close. Let's do this!

Chapter Two

SUPERHERO DEACTIVATORS

YOU DON'T HAVE TO CHANGE A MAN TO INSPIRE HIM. YOU SIMPLY HAVE TO AWAKEN THE HERO ALREADY INSIDE HIM.

SOLO TO SOULMATE REFLECTIONS

Did you know that, according to research from the National Institutes of Health, the top three causes of divorce are:

- Lack of commitment *(this ranks as #1).*
- Too much arguing and unresolved conflict (which erodes intimacy).
- Infidelity.

As my husband David wisely says, *"Little keys unlock big doors, and big doors swing on small hinges."*

In other words, our actions in the small moments often determine the outcomes in the big ones.

Often it starts quietly with: A sigh. An eyeroll. A weary tone that says more than words ever could.

Most women don't even realize when they're doing it. I know I didn't.

But over time, these subtle signals begin to build a silent wall. And the superhero spirit inside a good man starts to power down, not because he stopped loving, but because he no longer feels safe to love freely.

Understanding the Superhero Instinct

Many women don't realize how superhero deactivators can repel a good man and quietly sour a good relationship.

In the chapters ahead, we'll take a deep dive into the various personality types and the subtle, often unintentional, man-breaking behaviors that can damage intimacy.

Throughout our lives, every woman has played or is currently playing the role of a superhero deactivator in some way... and she doesn't even realize it.

That was me. What about you?

There are times when women intentionally engage in superhero deactivators for different reasons.

Sometimes it could be that a man or someone in the past hurt her, and she won't allow healing in her soul.

Other times, she doesn't realize how her words, tone, actions, etc. are negatively impacting him. And other times, it's a form of revenge. Regardless of the reason, the results are the same and he's damaged in various ways, such as the examples in the previous chapter. Typically, soul wounds are the root in these WIIFM behaviors.

Every good man is wired with a God-given instinct:

- Protect
- Provide
- Pursue

When a man feels like he can win with you, that his efforts matter, that his heart is received and respected, he rises.

But when he feels he can't win, no matter how hard he tries, he slowly pulls back.

Never forget: the most important opinion in the world to a man is his queen's.

Women Unknowingly Deactivate Their Man's Inner Hero

Without realizing it, women can sometimes send silent but painful messages:

- *"I don't need you."*
- *"You're doing it wrong."*
- *"You're not good enough."*

And it's not always through loud arguments. More often, it's through:

- Sarcasm
- Criticism
- Eyerolls
- *"Helpful"* corrections that land as disrespect

My Pillsbury Doughboy Moment

Small moments matter, more than we think.

They can tip the scale of a relationship in one direction or another, sometimes permanently.

After one of our separations, Mr. Wrong was trying, truly trying. He was more attentive, more thoughtful.

It felt unfamiliar to me. Although I had longed for that change, something inside me hadn't caught up.

I was still angry: Still hurting and it showed.

One day, I told him he needed to lose weight.

Not for his health, but for payback.

Here's the back story:

He had spent months picking apart my body. Telling me to dye my hair blonde. Making comments about my *"saggy"* butt. Pressuring me to get a breast job. (Which I never got.)

So, when I poked his large Buddha belly and mockingly called him the *"Pillsbury Doughboy,"* complete with sound effects, it wasn't about love.

It was a jab.

It was a cheap shot, straight from the vault of unforgiveness.

I thought I was being funny. But the truth? It was cruel. A putdown is a putdown, whether it's subtle or blatant. At other times, I nitpicked everything he did. How he folded the laundry. How he held the steering wheel. How he made the bed. Eventually, he stopped trying. He deflated like a balloon losing air.

Because here's the truth:

When a man feels like he can't win with you, he'll stop trying. Back then, I didn't realize I was wielding my pain like an ice pick:

Each complaint. Each sarcastic jab. Each *"justified"* joke.

It wasn't love. It was revenge and revenge is just sabotage in disguise.

You're doing such brave work right now, so proud of you for pressing in! You're uncovering your inner diamond, layer by layer, truth by truth.

Now, let's take a closer look at some important superhero deactivators, so we can stop chipping away at the love we desire, and start building the kind of connection that lasts.

Superhero Deactivators	What It Feels Like to Him
Criticizing how he does things:	*"I can't do anything right."*
Constantly correcting him:	*"She doesn't trust me."*
Interrupting or talking over him:	*"My voice doesn't matter."*
Dismissing his efforts:	*"Why bother trying?"*
Mocking or subtle put downs in public or private:	*"I'm being disrespected."*
Acting like you don't need him:	*"There's no place for me in her life."*

Understanding is the Beginning of Knowledge

- When a man feels respected and appreciated, he rises into his best self.
- When he feels criticized and dismissed, he retreats to protect himself.
- You don't inspire a man by managing him. You inspire him by believing in and affirming him.

Introducing the Man Mirror

Here's something powerful:

The way YOU see a man often becomes the way HE sees himself.

This is what I call, *The Man Mirror.*

- See him as capable, and he strives to become more capable.
- See him as incompetent, and he'll shrink back and shut down.
- See him as heroic, and he'll rise to meet that vision, stepping into the best version of himself.

Let me ask you a few questions.

What mirror are you holding up to your man, or to a good Mr. Potential?

What mirror did you hold up in past relationships?

And here's the most important question of all:

Does your perspective need to shift in any way?

When the Man Mirror Is Broken: Julie's Story

One of my coaching clients, we'll call her Julie, came to me after 15 years of marriage. She was frustrated and heartbroken, saying:

"My husband isn't a leader. He doesn't take initiative. I have to tell him everything, how to discipline the kids, how to manage the house... even basic things like making sure the bills get paid."

Julie felt disillusioned. She longed for a strong leader, a true *"head of the household."*

But as we explored her story more deeply, a painful truth came to the surface:

She didn't realize that her man mirror, her constant instructing, correcting, controlling, and micromanaging had slowly eroded his confidence.

Over time, her husband's behaviors began to reflect the very image she held of him.

When she was coached to make changes and affirm his efforts, she refused, insisting he should take initiative without needing affirmation.

Here's what was really happening:

- Julie's husband was naturally soft-spoken and thoughtful. He needed encouragement.
- But her frustrated tone, snarky remarks, and endless critiques made him feel incapable, inept, and unneeded.
- He had lost all confidence.
- Her man mirror reflected a man who couldn't think for himself, who was slow, and who failed at even simple tasks. His actions reflected her mirror.

Now imagine if Julie had chosen a different mirror.

- Imagine if she celebrated even the smallest wins and affirmed him.
- Imagine if she praised his efforts instead of highlighting every flaw.
- Imagine if she softened her tone and chose encouragement over frustration.

What would have happened? Her husband could have blossomed into the leader she prayed for—not because he changed overnight, but because he felt trusted and believed in.

A man rises when he knows he is seen, valued, and supported by his queen.

But sadly, Julie wasn't willing to look at herself. Everything was his fault.

She received an emotional payoff by staying trapped in her circle of resentment, anger, and unforgiveness.

Remember this, beautiful:

Your words hold power, and your presence sets the tone.

And the way you carry your man's heart publicly and privately will either crown him... or quietly crush him.

Let's look at another example.

The Cackling Hens

Ever wonder how a man tells his wife of 25 years that he wants a divorce?

One evening, David and I slipped away to a beautiful restaurant, where chandeliers sparkled and soft music wrapped around the candlelight like a warm embrace. It was the kind of evening that invited connection and romance.

Until two couples sat down at the table beside us, and the music, at least emotionally, came to a screeching halt.

It didn't take long to figure out who held the mic at their table. Take a guess. Yep, the wives. Their loud, grating tones could irritate even the sweetest nun on the planet. It was nonstop chatter. Talk, talk, talk...like cackling hens.

Have you ever met people like that?

They dominated the conversation with endless complaints, about their kids, their friends, and yes, their husbands, who were sitting right there. And anything else they could critique.

Any attempt from the men to join the conversation was met with dismissal or interruption, and they were talked over.

The husbands just sat quietly, eyes glazed over.

They were kind. They were respectful. They were invisible.

I watched one of the men attempt a lighthearted comment. His wife swatted it away without a second glance and rolled into another rant. She didn't even notice the silent retreat on his face.

What struck me most wasn't just the volume and tone of their voices:

It was the men's mental disconnect. It was a slow emotional divorce happening over dinner.

Clearly, this had been happening for years.

These men weren't angry. They were resigned.

They were unseen and unheard. Slowly fading in real time.

And I found myself wondering: What must their at home life be like?

Sometimes, it's not one big betrayal that breaks a man's heart. It's a thousand small cuts that occur over time, in public and private.

Do I believe those women meant to harm their husbands? Probably not.

Do I believe they were even aware of what they were doing? Sadly, no.

Would they be willing to change if someone pointed it out? Maybe, but not likely.

Queen in the making, let this be your wake-up call. Come into awareness about your words. Your tone, your attitude.

Find intentional ways, both big and small, to honor your man in public and in private.

Speak with grace. Choose kindness. Let your words reflect the queen you are becoming.

Because the way you carry your man's heart in front of others... matters.

What I Call the Powerful *Man Mirror*

The mirror you hold up shapes the man standing before you.

- Reflect honor, and he rises.
- Reflect criticism, and he withdraws.
- Reflect belief, and he dares to lead.

Here's the amazing part: the *Man Mirror* doesn't just shift your relationship with men; it transforms how you see yourself. You begin to understand that you are a woman, powerful enough to inspire greatness.

When I met my husband David, I was finally in the heart-space where I could:

- Speak to the king inside of him, not the critic.
- Honor his small acts of leadership, not dismiss them.
- Create a safe emotional environment, where love could grow and thrive.

But what about real problems? What about healthy standards and accountability?

Absolutely, they matter. **A queen doesn't abandon her standards; she elevates the way she communicates them**. More to come on that!

There's a big difference between expressing your needs with grace and tearing someone down through criticism or contempt. That's why, in the chapters ahead, we'll dive into Emotional Intelligence *(what I call the EQ Factor)* and how to level up your skills to address issues in a queenly, powerful way, without damage.

Remember: Bridges build connection. Walls build loneliness. Choose the bridge.

Optional Reflection Prayer

Lord, teach me to hold up mirrors of honor, not judgment. Show me how to see others, and myself, the way You do: through eyes of love, strength, and redemption. Prepare my heart to reflect beauty and inspire greatness. Amen.

Ready for What's Next?

Now, it's time to turn the mirror toward someone else: **You**.

In the next chapter, you'll meet the most beautiful reflection you've ever seen... your true self, waiting to be fully known and deeply loved.

You'll also discover one of the most common issues women face that unknowingly repels love, and how to gently shift it.

Let's do this, beautiful!

Practical Application

1. Reflect: List specific examples of Superhero Deactivators you've engaged in during past relationships. Describe what you said, did, and the result of those.

2. Activate Kindness:

This week, practice intentional kindness toward someone who has made a mistake, whether big or small.

Perform three random acts of kindness or speak gentle, encouraging words to someone who might typically be corrected, judged, or dismissed.

Here's the Catch:

- Do not point out their mistake(s).
- Do not correct them.

Instead, respond with grace. Offer encouragement. Extend understanding. Maybe it's a co-worker who dropped the ball. Maybe it's your child, your partner, or a stranger.

Then, reflect on your experience:

How did you feel choosing kindness over correction?

What thoughts or emotions came up for you?

Was there an *"Aha!"* moment? If so, what was it?

How did the person respond to being treated with kindness instead of criticism?

What did you notice in yourself after responding this way?

Share your story! We'd love to hear about your experience inside our private Solo to Soulmate Sisterhood community.

Your story might be just what another sister needs to hear.

Let's keep encouraging each other, one breakthrough at a time.

Now it's time to journal your Practical Application homework.

Use the lines below to reflect on what you've learned and how it's shifting your mindset and behavior.

_____

_____

_____

_____

_____

_____

_____

_____

_____

_____

_____

_____

_____

_____

_____

_____

_____

_____

_____

_____

Journal Reflections

- In the past, how have my words, actions, or reactions unknowingly shaped how the men in my life saw themselves?

- What would it look like if I chose to reflect encouragement instead of criticism? What would shift in me, and in them?

- How can I begin applying the Man Mirror principle, not just in romantic relationships, but in every interaction with friends, family, coworkers, or even strangers?

- When I think about the men in my life, past or present, what kind of mirror have I been holding up? One of belief and honor… or one of disappointment and judgment?

- If I chose to consistently reflect belief, encouragement, and honor, how might my relationships begin to transform?

- What simple, daily actions can I start taking to help a good man rise instead of retreat?

_____

_____

_____

_____

_____

_____

_____

_____

_____

_____

_____

_____

_____

_____

_____

_____

_____

_____

_____

_____

_____

_____

_____

_____

_____

_____

_____

_____

_____

_____

_____

_____

_____

Heart Reflections
FROM JOANNA

I'm so proud of you, Queen!

You've just completed a powerful turning point in your love journey.

Take a moment and ask yourself: *What man mirror have I been holding up?*

Your words, your energy, and the way you see a man have the power to inspire greatness—or quietly push him away. Simply being aware of this sets you apart from so many women.

It's about choosing new ways to love. That means tiny words, subtle tones, and simple gestures often matter more than we realize.

Your Man Mirror can inspire a man to rise, lead, and love deeply—or cause him to withdraw and shut down.

And today, you've begun stepping into your incredible power: the power to become a woman who builds bridges, not walls.

Ready for the next foundation stone in the next chapter?

Now that you've learned how your mirror toward others can shape a relationship…it's time to turn that mirror inward to the beautiful **YOU**.

Chapter Three

THE BEAUTIFUL YOU

> *THE MIRROR CAN ONLY REFLECT WHAT THE HEART BELIEVES.*
> SOLO TO SOULMATE REFLECTIONS

W hen you're alone in front of the mirror... what do you really see?

- Do you feel beautiful?
- Do you feel like you're enough?
- Do old voices whisper lies of unworthiness?
- Do you focus on the flaws, not the beauty?

Let's Dig a Little Deeper...

Have you secretly battled perfectionism, struggled to feel worthy, or wrestled with body shame or aging fears?

Do you have a hard time receiving compliments without deflecting it?

Do the words *"If only I were this"* or *"If only I were that"* constantly wage war in your mind?

If you answered *"Yes"* to any of these, you are not alone. I've been there too.

But here's the good news, you can shift your inner mirror.

You can rewrite your reflection. You can learn to fall in love with the beautiful you.

There was quite a bit of trauma I had to work through after my marriage to Mr. Wrong. And the first step was learning to shift my inner mirror, how I saw myself, and then learning how to receive. We'll go deeper into both of those as we move forward.

Why the Inner Mirror Matters

We've already talked about the power of the Man Mirror, but now it's time to turn inward.

What does your inner mirror reflect about YOU?

Is the image you show the world different from the one you carry on the inside?

As we journey from solo to soulmate, your inner thoughts and self-talk become the foundation we build on next. These reflections shape your identity and how you interact with life and love.

Your Inner Mirror Influences:

- How you interpret other people's actions.
- How you respond emotionally.
- How you make decisions in love, friendship, and opportunity.

At its core, your self-image determines your confidence, your worth, your energy, and your ability to receive real love.

Your mindset about yourself, and how you speak to yourself literally shapes your world.

Words Build Up or Words Tear Down

As women, we often don't hear enough of what's true: that we are radiant, strong, beautiful, and deeply valuable. Instead, many of us grow up with the opposite words that wounded, voices that criticized, or silences that left us wondering if we mattered at all.

Words can build destiny... or destroy it. Many women have heard more tearing down than lifting up.

Maybe you can relate to one of these:

- A father who was absent, critical, or controlling.
- A mother whose love came with conditions.
- A bully who sowed seeds of shame and rejection.
- An ex who chipped away at your worth with every betrayal or careless word.
- Or maybe just years of emotional neglect.

These wounds often form the *"old tapes,"* subconscious messages that play over and over. And when new hurtful moments occur, they only reinforce those old beliefs.

Over time, this shapes how you see yourself, and even how you accept (or reject) something as simple as a compliment.

Our identity as women can be stolen. And when that happens, our inner mirror, our sense of confidence, self-worth, and self-respect, becomes distorted.

We start believing lies about ourselves:

"I'm ugly."

"I'm not smart enough."

"I'm not good enough."

"I'm not pretty enough."

"I have to perform, prove, or earn love to be worthy of it."

These false beliefs often become the emotional root of how we respond to others, through jealousy, control, backstabbing, manipulation, or even lies.

Why? Because wounded people wound people. Hurting people hurt people.

And often, the ones who bear the brunt of those wounds are the good men in our lives, men who never caused the pain but feel the ripple effect of our unhealed places.

What's the deeper root of unhealthy behaviors?

Most often, it's this: Unhealed hurt. Unforgiveness. Bitterness. Trauma, whether big or small.

It's pain we've buried. Shame we've swallowed.

It's the parts of our story we never processed or let God heal.

As a coach and speaker, I've walked alongside countless women.

More often than not, the same two core wounds surface: *a broken mirror of identity*, and *an inability to receive love without shame or resistance.*

These two often lie at the root of so much emotional dysfunction.

My Healing Began When I Chose to Receive

One of the very first steps in my own healing journey was learning to receive love and forgive myself.

Was it easy? Not at all.

But I made myself do it. And I want to help you do the same.

If you feel like you need extra prayer support, go to Appendix A at the back of this book. There's a healing prayer waiting for you there.

And if more things start surfacing, and you want to go deeper, I invite you to join our private Solo to Soulmate Sisterhood Facebook group. It's a safe, sacred space filled with courageous women just like you.

You are not broken. You're a diamond being polished.

Here's the truth:

Nothing is too messy, too painful, or too complicated for God. Not your past. Not your heartbreak. Not your hidden wounds.

You are healing. You are transforming. Truly, it begins by shifting what you believe and say about yourself.

For me, the most powerful shift came when I invited God into the process.

I asked my heavenly Father to heal my broken inner mirror and replace it with a divine reflection of His unconditional love through His eyes.

That's when everything began to change, my confidence, my heart, and ultimately, my love story.

I still had to do the work, but God healed the wounds.

He helped me:

- Restore my royal identity.
- Break the lies I had believed.
- Rewrite my inner story, from shame to strength, from self-doubt to dignity.

These inner transformations changed my love story outcomes.

In my coaching program, we explore this healing process in greater depth. But for now, let this chapter be your sacred beginning.

Ask yourself.

- What am I saying to myself every day?
- What lies have I believed?
- What negative labels or declarations am I still carrying?
- What mirror am I holding up to my own heart?

Here's the good news:

You are receiving practical tools to begin transforming your inner mirror, so that it reflects truth, wholeness, and radiant beauty again.

My husband David once shared a powerful study with me that beautifully illustrates everything we've been talking about.

Ready for something eye-opening?

Let's dive in.

The Scar Experiment

In a fascinating psychological study, women were told the experiment was about how facial disfigurement affects public perception.

Using special-effects makeup, researchers created highly realistic scars on each woman's face. Each woman was then shown her *"scar"* in the mirror before heading into a mock job interview.

But here's the twist.

Right before the interview, the makeup artist pretended to do a final *"touch-up"* and secretly removed the scar. The women didn't know. They believed the scar was still on their face.

The result?

- Every woman entered her interview believing she was disfigured.
- Almost all of them reported feeling judged, rejected, or treated harshly, despite the fact that there was no scar at all.

Why?

Because they **believed** they were flawed.

And that belief shaped the way they showed up, and how they perceived every interaction.

Perception shapes experience. Your inner mirror shapes your outer world.

Their distorted self-image colored their confidence, their body language, their tone of voice, and even the way they interpreted other people's reactions. They walked into the room expecting judgment, and so they found evidence of it, even when it wasn't really there.

Have you ever done that?

Have you ever assumed rejection, criticism, or unworthiness before anyone said a word?

This is the quiet power of the inner mirror.

The way you see yourself directly affects the energy you carry, and what you believe you deserve.

How to Retrain Your Inner Mirror

Ready to start reshaping the way you see yourself?

Let's begin with a simple, but powerful exercise.

For the next 5 days, stand about six feet away from a mirror. Look yourself in the eyes and speak these affirmations out loud and with energy:

"I am beautiful. I am loved. God loves me. I attract healthy, godly love. I am successful and worthy of it."

Why six feet?

Because at that distance, you're not fixated on flaws. You don't zoom in on pores or wrinkles. You see your full self, whole, radiant, loved.

There's research that shows spoken affirmations can rewire your brain, shift your emotional frequency, and transform the way you engage with the world.

The Power of Words

Words carry weight. They create or destroy. Bless or curse. Heal or harm.

Some of us have lived under word curses, careless, cutting statements spoken by others or even by ourselves. But that can change today.

You can begin to receive words of truth, healing, and blessing.

Are you ready to receive yours?

According to the Merriam-Webster Dictionary, a blessing is *"the act or words of one that blesses."*

So right now, I invite you to receive a blessing.

Place your hand over your heart and speak this aloud:

"I give myself permission to receive my blessing."

And if you need to add this: *"and to forgive myself."*

> **HE WILL AGAIN HAVE COMPASSION ON US,**
> **AND WILL SUBDUE OUR INIQUITIES.**
> **YOU WILL CAST ALL OUR SINS**
> **INTO THE DEPTHS OF THE SEA.**
> MICAH 7:19 NKJV

Because here's the truth:

God forgives you. He has compassion for you. If you've made mistakes, the first step toward healing is to forgive yourself and let go.

Now say it again, but this time with energy! (This is key).

"I give myself permission to receive my blessing!"

And now... SHOUT it with joyful boldness! (Go on, YELL it!).

"I give myself permission to receive my blessing!"

Say it from deep in your belly. Let your entire body feel it. Your words carry life. Your agreement with truth shifts the atmosphere.

Now, open your hands. Take a deep breath. And receive this, read it out loud as if I'm speaking directly to your heart:

"I speak healing over your soul, your heart, your mind, and your body.

I break off every negative word ever spoken over you. I declare that you are beautiful, inside and out.

You are worthy. You are accepted, loved, honored, and cherished. You are forgiven.

You are strong and courageous. There is everything right about you. In Jesus name. Amen."

Let these words sink in. Let them soften the broken places. Breathe them in until they become part of your new truth.

Note: You can also speak these words using *"I"* instead of *"you."*

Return to this declaration as often as you need. **Also, feel free to go to Appendix A for additional prayers of healing.**

A Royal Reminder

Did you know that the definition of *"Princess"* is one who stands strong and courageous, one who takes dominion over her land?

Yes, Beautiful. That's you.

Maybe you've never thought of yourself as a princess. Maybe you thought princesses had to look a certain way or live in a fairy tale. But the truth is, a real princess, a daughter of the King stands strong in battle. She leads with wisdom. She reclaims her territory.

And you, beloved, are doing just that.

By being open. By choosing change. By letting God rewrite your story.

I am so proud of you!

I invite you to reflect on this new royal identity. Think about all the times in your life you had to be strong or courageous, even when no one else saw it. Even when you did it scared.

Your Inner Dialogue Shapes Your Destiny

What you believe, what you expect, what you speak, it all colors the way you show up in love, and how others respond to you.

We saw this clearly in the Scar Experiment.

That's why your declarations matter. They're not just positive affirmations; they're a spiritual reset. A new frequency. A rewiring of truth.

It's a mindset shift that says:

"I'm no longer walking in rejection, fear, or old programming.

I'm walking in power. In purpose. In the mindset of a Queen."

I'm going to teach you an additional exercise that helped shift my mindset on multiple levels. You may or may not be familiar with it. **Remember, awareness is the key to change.**

You're going to identify the negative thoughts or beliefs about yourself, discredit it and create a new belief. Then consistently speak it out.

This method helped positively shift my mindset about everything from relationships to finances. Throughout the day, I jotted down all the negative thoughts that went through my mind.

When I reviewed the list, I stared in disbelief at the pages and pages of negativity.

Healing is both spiritual and practical. This life-changing exercise helped me rewire my thinking in any situation and I still occasionally do it to this day.

Changing the Inner Mirror **Technique Step-by-Step**

- Write down every negative thought you notice throughout the day. Don't filter, just observe and record.

- Counter each one with a positive, empowering truth.
- Renounce the lie aloud.
- Declare the new truth aloud, with passion and boldness from deep in your belly!

You are retraining your brain. You are reprogramming your heart. You are breaking agreement with lies and choosing to walk in truth.

Let's look at an example together in the next section.

Example: Transforming Your Inner Mirror

Use the table below as a guide to begin retraining your inner thoughts. You are replacing toxic lies with life-giving truth. **This isn't just positive thinking; this is spiritual alignment.** This is you agreeing with Heaven over your identity and future.

Negative Thought	Positive Thought	New Declaration
"All the good men are taken."	*"I attract emotionally healthy, available men."*	*"I renounce the lie that all the good men are taken! I attract great men of character and heart."*
"I'm not pretty enough."	*"I am uniquely beautiful, inside and out."*	*"I renounce the lie that I am not enough. I am radiant, strong, and deeply loved."*

Speak your new declarations out loud and with authority. Let your body, your mind, and your spirit come into agreement with what God says about you.

50

Example Declaration:

"I renounce and come out of agreement with the lie that all the good guys are taken! I attract available, emotionally healthy men of character and heart!"

This is part of the powerful process of creating awareness and retraining your brain. Your words shape your world, and your agreement matters. When you replace lies with truth, you begin to shift your inner mirror and change what you attract.

So, stand tall, beautiful!

You are royalty, a princess in God's Kingdom, strong, radiant, and boldly taking dominion over your life.

Receiving your true identity is not arrogance, it's humility: an agreement with Heaven about who you really are.

Healthy Self-Love isn't Selfish, It's Sacred

If you've ever struggled with putting everyone else first at the cost of yourself, you're not alone.

Women are natural nurturers. We're mothers caring for our children. We are church volunteers feeding the homeless or the daughters looking after aging parents.

We're taught it's better to give than to receive, and while that's a beautiful principle, it can become deeply imbalanced. It did for me.

Women with mercy hearts, the nurturers, the caretakers, often slip into codependence, believing it's selfish to receive love, rest, or restoration.

But here's the truth:

You are worthy of care. You are worthy of healing. You are worthy of love.

I can't stress enough how powerful it is to begin the healing process of learning how to love yourself, to forgive yourself, receive grace, and walk in compassion for your own heart.

There was such freedom when I gave myself permission to:

- Extend myself grace.
- Honor my courage.
- Embrace my weaknesses with empathy.
- Appreciate the qualities that make me unique and special.
- Believe that all things are possible, even for me.

This is the mindset shift from poverty to royalty:

"I'm no longer walking in rejection, fear, or past programming. I'm walking in power, in God's purpose, and in the mindset of a queen."

And as I embraced these truths, something incredible happened. I began to teach others how to love, honor, and respect me.

> *HOW YOU LOVE YOURSELF TEACHES OTHERS HOW TO LOVE YOU.*
> RUPI KAUR

Mirror, What Do You See?

Imagine looking in the mirror and finally seeing what's already there:

- Beauty
- Courage
- Radiance
- Worth
- Hope

This isn't just a dream, it's your destiny when you commit to the healing path.

You're doing it, beautiful! And the best part?

Your real love story is just beginning.

In the next chapter, you'll unlock one of the most underrated but powerful skills for lasting love, *Emotional Intelligence*. It's a superpower most women are never taught, but it holds the keys to deeper connection, understanding, and joy.

Are you ready to turn the page with me? Let's go!

Journal Reflections

- What old voices still echo in your inner mirror?
- What new truths do you want to replace them with?
- How would your life shift if you lived from a healed, radiant self-image?

Reflection Prayer

Heavenly Father,

Heal my inner mirror. Teach me to see myself the way You see me, beautiful, courageous, worthy, and loved.

Help me break agreement with every lie from the past. Prepare my heart to walk in new love, new joy, and a renewed identity. Amen.

Practical Application

Now it's your turn. The next page has a thought tracker to help create awareness of the negative thoughts and counter them with a positive truth.

In the tracker write down your:

- Negative thoughts (the lies you've believed)
- Positive truths (what God says about you)
- The new declarations, also spoken out loud, boldly and from the gut!
- Then you'll say them daily. Say them loudly.

Speak life into your inner mirror, and into your future.

You've got this. We're doing it together!

Negative Thought	Positive Thought	New Declaration

Heart Reflections

Breathe this in, beautiful one.

You just crossed a major milestone in your transformation journey. *How did it feel to bless yourself today?*

You gave yourself permission to receive.
You chose to go deeper.
You began seeing yourself with compassion.

These aren't small wins—they're life-changing shifts that open the door to new love and new beginnings.

You've learned the power of words, the practice of replacing old lies, and the art of rewriting your inner mirror with truth. Every time you speak life over yourself, your heart listens. Every time you agree with Heaven's perspective, you rise.

Now, Queen… are you ready for the next master key—Emotional Intelligence? In the next chapter, we'll explore how even brilliant women can get stuck when their EQ hasn't fully grown.

Get ready! Good men will begin gravitating toward you with ease.

Chapter Four

THE HIDDEN LOVE SUPERPOWER
(The EQ Factor-Emotional Intelligence)

> *BEHIND AN ANGRY WOMAN STANDS A MAN WHO HAS*
> *ABSOLUTELY NO IDEA WHAT HE DID WRONG.*
> UNKNOWN

It's funny because it's true: how many times have you seen a friend fuming because her man didn't *just know* what she was thinking?

How often have you caught yourself assuming someone should be able to read your mind?

We've all been there, expecting someone to *"get it"* without us ever expressing it. And when they don't, we react with frustration, passive-aggressive behaviors, withdrawal, or worse, hurtful words we can't take back.

As we discussed earlier, there are two sides to every relationship coin.

One side reflects the choices and behaviors of men. The other side reflects our choices as women.

We are courageously flipping the coin to our side, not to blame ourselves, but to heal, to grow, and to level up.

Before we go deeper, let's pause and reflect on these questions:

- Do you react or respond when you feel hurt?
- Do you accuse or ask with curiosity?

- Do you hint or clearly express your needs?
- Do you assume or seek understanding?
- Do you ignore hurtful behavior or lovingly hold it accountable?

Your honest answers are the starting point for massive breakthroughs.

Great job, you're showing up with intention!

Let's recap some powerful truths we've already explored:

- The **WIIFM** Syndrome *(What's In It For Me?)*, and how it blocks real love.
- The power of receiving blessings and the impact of the words we speak, about ourselves and others.
- How to transform negative thoughts into life-giving truth to retrain your mind.
- How the *Man Mirror* reflects our emotional health and mindset back to us.

Now, let's tackle one of the most important, overlooked superpowers in relationships.

It's called **Emotional Intelligence, the *EQ Factor*.** Developing emotional maturity in the *EQ factor* arena can change your entire world.

So, what is Emotional Intelligence *(EQ Factor)*? I'm glad you asked.

EQ is the capacity to be aware of, understand, and manage your own emotions, and also recognize and respond to the emotions of others.

Emotional intelligence is about the *way* we communicate and it increases our ability to do so.

Here's What EQ Looks Like in Action:

- Recognizing and regulating your own emotions (instead of being ruled by them).
- Understanding and respecting the emotions of others, without *personalizing* everything.
- Communicating clearly, kindly, and honestly.
- Resolving conflict without escalating drama.
- Setting healthy boundaries without guilt, shame, or fear.

_EQ_ Was a Game-Changer in My Love Journey

One of the biggest breakthroughs in my shift from solo to soulmate was developing my emotional maturity. The more I grew in my identity and *EQ*, the smoother my relationships became.

Did my EQ maturity happen overnight? No, it didn't. It took time to become aware of triggers, grow and mature in my communication skills.

Growing in emotional intelligence isn't about being perfect, it's about progress.

It's about being intentional with your responses. Does this take practice?

Yes, combined with a willingness to acknowledge those harder to accept truths about us. Our culture tends to deny truth and bury things in the sand like an ostrich.

It's about flying like an eagle, not hiding the head in the sand like the ostrich.

When challenges arise, the ostrich hides from conflict, hoping it disappears. The eagle faces challenges, soars higher to suffocate fear or remove its enemy. Many of us tend to hide like the ostrich. The key is being aware. Then make changes.

Be encouraged, because you are leveling up your love game!

A few reflection questions…

- Where have you acted like an ostrich or an eagle in various relationships and situations?
- What are your automatic responses when you're triggered, angry or disappointed?
- Where is God inviting you to rise, emotionally, relationally, and spiritually?

Let's Talk *Code Speak* vs. *Clear Speak*

Do you talk in code or clearly voice your needs?

The woman who knows how to lovingly speak her truth is the woman who gets heard, honored, and cherished.

That kind of woman walks in courage, like the eagle we talked about earlier.

But many of us unknowingly fall into what I call the *"Code Speak."* trap.

It's a subtle language of dropping hints, hoping someone will pick up on what we really want or need without us having to say it directly.

We talk in code. And then we wonder why our needs aren't being met and feel frustrated.

Here Are a Few Common Examples of Code Speak:

- *"Wow, it must be nice to relax while I clean."*

(Translation: I'm overwhelmed and hoping you'll offer to help.)

- *"I saw the cutest necklace today."*

(Translation: I really want that necklace for my birthday. If you loved me, you'd remember it for my birthday next month.)

- *"There's a nice pile of laundry waiting to be washed...?"*

(Translation: I want you to do laundry or at least offer to help.)

Instead of clearly communicating what we need, we hint, sigh, or make side comments, expecting him to *just know*.

We assume love equals mind reading. But here's the truth, beautiful one: Men don't speak in hints. They speak in headlines.

They need clarity. Not sarcasm, not passive jabs and not riddles.

When we use *Code Speak*, we often feel unseen and unloved.

It's not because he doesn't care, but because he wasn't given a chance to meet real needs.

Clear Speak is what emotionally intelligent women use.

It means:

- You express your needs lovingly and directly.
- You take ownership of your emotions without blaming.
- You invite connections instead of demanding compliance.

When he magically doesn't know what we want, we get upset. We feel hurt.

But here's the truth: He can't read your mind. Learning to clearly communicate your needs and desires is a vital part of increasing your *EQ Factor*.

Here's the truth: Clarity is kindness.

As women, we tend to buy into the lie that we must hint at our needs, or we may not get what we're asking for.

We don't realize that love is not a guessing game for others to try and decipher.

Clear Speak uses clear, kind communication that builds safety, not distance. It increases love and connection. It doesn't push love away. It protects it. It creates emotional safety. It fosters trust. It invites vulnerability.

In contrast, Code Speak often stems from fear. A fear of being too much, too needy, or easily rejected. Sometimes, it's rooted in unresolved pain from past relationships or unmet childhood needs.

But here's the beautiful truth, Queen:

A healthy, emotionally mature man won't be intimidated by your clarity. He will welcome it. He'll respect your honesty. He'll love your confidence. He'll appreciate that you express your heart with kindness and maturity, without blame, drama, or manipulation.

That kind of woman stands out. That kind of woman invites lasting love. These are the skills help a woman be heard and seen in a healthy way.

EQ Skill Upgrade Time

Imagine being able to have hard conversations without emotional chaos.

Imagine your partner responding in calm, healthy ways instead of the unhealthy reactions you may have experienced in the past.

Coming up in this chapter, you'll find a guide for healthier EQ responses — simple, powerful ways to communicate with clarity, confidence, and emotional maturity.

Let's take a look at some of the top emotional intelligence (EQ) skills we want to develop.

Common EQ (emotional intelligence) skills we want to develop are:

Skill	Meaning
Self-awareness	Recognizing your emotions and triggers. Learn to respond differently to those triggers.
Self-regulation	Calming yourself before reacting.
Empathy	Understanding your partner's feelings without judgment. Not dismissing their feelings.
Stress management	Staying steady under pressure and conflict. Learn techniques to reduce triggers.
Boundaries	Expressing what's okay and not okay, lovingly. Saying "no" with grace.
Social skills	Handling tough conversations with wisdom and lovingly speaking the truth.

Isn't this enlightening?

Before we move on, I'd be remiss not to bring up a subject many women have struggled with at some point in their lives, the infamous *"It's that time of the month!"* excuse for poor behavior.

Yes, hormones, (whether menstrual or menopausal) can significantly affect our emotions. And yes, there are many natural alternatives that can help support balance. *(Check out Appendix B for alternative information. Personally, frequency therapy played a big role in my own healing journey.)*

But here's the truth: Hormonal shifts are never a free pass card to mistreat others.

I once watched a woman scream at her husband in a store because their child accidentally broke something. She was the parent standing closest to the child, yet she lashed out at her husband, and when others stared in disbelief, she shrugged and said, *"I'm on my period."*

Let me say this gently but firmly…

Blaming, shaming, and emotional dumping erode trust.

Emotional maturity means taking ownership of our responses, even when it's hard. Even when we're tired, overwhelmed, or in pain. And especially when someone else's heart is on the line.

When Reactions Don't Match the Moment

Ever felt yourself overreacting and wondered, *"Why did I just say that? Why did that hurt sooo much?"*

That moment of intensity is often a red light, a divine signal inviting us to pause and ask:

"Lord, what's really going on inside of me right now?"

In my own life, I've discovered that most overreactions are rooted in deeper issues, unhealed wounds, unmet emotional needs, or buried unforgiveness.

But here's the good news: God doesn't shame you for your reactions.

He meets you in them. He gently shines light on the deeper root and invites you into healing.

Can we all have moments when our emotional intelligence drops to zero? Absolutely. It happens to the best of us.

The goal is **not** perfection. The goal is awareness, ownership, and growth.

You are well on your way.

Real-World Emotional Lessons from Brilliant Women

You can be wildly successful, in business, creativity, or intellect, and still struggle in love because your emotional intelligence *(EQ)* hasn't caught up.

Let's take a look at a few iconic women from history whose various *EQ* challenges shaped their love lives:

Marilyn Monroe, Beauty and Brokenness

Marilyn was married three times, and each relationship ended in deep emotional pain. Despite her fame and charisma, Marilyn carried unhealed childhood wounds that led her into patterns of abandonment, emotional volatility, and painful dependency on men. Her beauty opened doors, but her inner world was crying out for safety and love.

Lesson: Unhealed emotional pain can sabotage even the brightest future.

Hedy Lamarr, The Lonely Genius

Hedy Lamarr, the Hollywood starlet turned inventor, was married six times. While she helped develop technology that led to Wi-Fi and Bluetooth, she remained isolated in love.

Hedy's brilliance couldn't compensate for her struggle to build emotional bonds. She lived in her headspace, not her heart space, and often intimidated men who didn't feel they could measure up. She didn't know how to draw out their inner superhero.

Lesson: Intellectual brilliance cannot replace emotional connection or relationship skills.

Elizabeth Taylor, The Queen of Turbulent Love

Married eight times (twice to Richard Burton), Elizabeth Taylor was magnetic, talented, and incredibly successful, yet her romantic life was full of drama and intensity.

She often fell *"in love with love,"* chasing emotional highs rather than stable, lasting connection. The drama, the chaos, and the whirlwind romance served a deeper need: to feel seen, validated, and emotionally significant.

Lesson: Emotional highs may feel thrilling, but they rarely lead to lasting love. It was all about her—**The WIIFM Syndrome**.

Let this be an encouragement, not a condemnation. These were powerful women with incredible strengths, but without emotional maturity, even greatness can unravel in relationships.

You're learning what many never do: how to pair emotional intelligence with spiritual truth. And that is a superpower.

Emotional maturity and healed hurts, not just passion, create lasting love.

Let me ask you something…

When someone disappoints you, how do you respond?

- Do you accuse or attack?
- Do you go silent and stew in passive-aggressive resentment?
- Do you explode in anger, or do you let things build up until you finally break?

Even when we seem to *"have it all,"* emotional intelligence isn't automatic. It doesn't come from degrees, success, or life experience alone. It comes from intentional growth, and it's a journey we continue walking, day by day.

True love doesn't begin by chasing the emotional high, it begins when you decide to heal your heart.

You can be a high-achieving, visionary woman, owning the boardroom, dazzling in the creative world, leading ministries, or raising amazing children.

Yet romantic relationships can be the one area where you feel stuck or overwhelmed. Why? Because intellect doesn't always equal emotional connection. *EQ* (emotional intelligence) is a skill that must be developed, like a muscle.

But here's the powerful part:

- You are doing something rare. Something brave.
- You're choosing growth. You're choosing healing. You're choosing intentional love.
- That is no small thing.
- You're breaking old patterns.
- You're rewriting your story.
- You're becoming the kind of woman who doesn't just dream about love: She attracts it.

> *BEING SMART DOESN'T MAKE YOU WISE. AND BRILLIANCE DOESN'T PROTECT YOU FROM HEARTBREAK, BUT WISDOM IS LIKE A DIAMOND.*
> UNKNOWN

Now Let's Talk Tone!

Tone can make or break a moment.
As women, especially when we're hurt or frustrated, we can slip into a tone that's snarky, sarcastic, dismissive, or accusatory, especially with the man we love. But nothing will send him into his emotional man cave faster than the wrong tone.

A major part of growing our emotional intelligence is learning to become aware of our tone, even in emotionally charged situations.

Can we work on our tone? Yes, we can.

Does it always come naturally? Not for most of us.

Is it possible to change? Absolutely.

Every day offers me a new opportunity to become more intentional with my words and how I say them. When triggers arise (and they will), I can choose to respond from love rather than react from pain. It takes practice, but it's powerful.

Let's walk through some common emotional traps, moments when overreacting could lead to disconnection, and discover better, more emotionally intelligent ways to handle them:

Forgotten Anniversary

Trigger: He forgets your anniversary.

Common Reaction: Exploding in rage: *"You don't love me!"*

EQ Response: Pause. Breathe. Then say,

"I feel really hurt that our anniversary was forgotten. Can we talk about what happened and how we can make each other feel more celebrated?"

Misinterpreted Text Message

Trigger: A female coworker texts your partner.

Common Reaction: Immediate accusation. *"You're cheating on me!"*

EQ Response: Take a breath. Respond gently:

"Hey, I noticed a message from someone. Can you share more about the context? It would give me a better understanding, and I don't jump to conclusions."

High-Stakes Meeting

Trigger: Someone criticizes your idea at work in a meeting.

Common Reaction: Getting defensive: *"How dare you question my idea! You're just jealous!"*

EQ Response: Breathe. Smile. Then respond with grace:

"Thanks for the feedback, I'll take some time to think about it."

(You stay composed, confident, and powerful.)

Managing the Moment: How to Stay Grounded

Breathing techniques can be your first line of defense when emotions begin to rise. If a response feels too intense in the moment, try a pattern interrupt, a quick physical shift that calms the nervous system and redirects your thoughts.

Here are a few simple, but powerful ways to reset your emotional state:

- Step outside for 60 seconds of fresh air.

- Shake out your arms or stretch.
- Splash cold water on your face.
- Take a brisk two-minute walk.
- Whisper a short prayer asking God for peace and clarity.

These small shifts help you re-center, respond wisely, and remain grounded in grace.

Important Note: This content is for educational and inspirational purposes only and is not a substitute for professional counseling or therapy. If you're navigating deep emotional challenges, please seek support from a trusted mental health professional.

As we grow in our emotional intelligence, the vocabulary we use begins to transform, and so do our relationships.

We may not be able to change someone else, but we can change how we respond. That's where our real power lies.

Most couples fall into communication patterns over time, like a familiar dance. When things feel rocky, it's easy to stay stuck in the same *wash-rinse-repeat cycle,* reacting the same way and getting the same results.

But what if you could interrupt that unhealthy pattern? What if, instead of reacting, you paused, and responded differently?

Good news: You can shift the dance. And it starts with small changes, like your choice of words and your tone.

To help you on this journey, I created a simple guide that compares low emotional intelligence *(EQ)* responses with higher *EQ* alternatives.

These word phrasing substitutions have been incredibly helpful in my own life, and I know they'll bless you too.

Let's take a look at a few examples together.

10-Word Substitution Guide for Healthier EQ Responses

This is a quick cheat sheet to instantly shift your emotional communication!

Instead of Saying...	Instead Try...
"You always..." / "You never..." (Accusatory)	*"Lately, I've noticed... Can we talk about it?"*
"Whatever." (Emotional distancing)	*"I need a moment to think about this."*
"Calm down." / "Relax." (Invalidates)	*"I see you're upset. How can I support you?"*
"You should..." (Controlling)	*"Would you be open to...?"*
"That's just how I am." (Avoids responsibility)	*"I'm working on this area. I know I can grow."*
"You make me feel..." (Blames others)	*"I feel... when... happens."*
"If you really loved me, you would..." (Manipulative)	*"What I need to feel loved right now is..."*
"Why are you so sensitive?" (Shames vulnerability)	*"That wasn't my intention. Can you share what you're feeling?"*
"I told you so." (Feeds ego, damages trust)	*"I understand how we got here. Let's figure out what's next."*
"It's not a big deal." (dismissive of others feelings)	*"It might not seem big to me, but I can see it matters to you."*

Remember This, Beautiful One:

Every time you pause instead of explode.

Every time you breathe instead of blame.

Every time you speak truth instead of code.

You are becoming the kind of woman who attracts and sustains healthy love. You're soaring higher. You're rewriting your legacy.

You're preparing for the king that Heaven has for you.

As we wrap up this chapter, let's get intentional about growing in our *EQ*.

Here are a few ways to begin:

1. Pause Before Reacting

When you feel really triggered, breathe in through your nose and out through your mouth. Do this a few times. Then, you can gently say to yourself:

"You've got this. Good recovery."

Let that breath become your bridge to composure. Repeat as needed.

2. Practice Empathy

Take a moment to see the situation from your partner's perspective. Ask yourself:

"What stress might he be carrying today?"

This shift softens your heart and strengthens your connection.

3. Develop Inquisitive, Not Accusation, Snarky or Sarcastic Tones.

Instead of slipping into a snarky, sarcastic, or accusatory tone, ask open-ended questions.

Try:

"Can you help me understand what you meant by that?"

Rather than:

"You always say things like that!"

4. Express Your Needs Clearly and Respectfully

Stop expecting him to read your mind. It's exhausting for both of you.

Use this formula instead:

"I feel [emotion] when [situation] happens. I need [specific action or support]."

Example:

"I feel overwhelmed when I have to manage dinner and the kids alone. I'd like us to come up with a better game plan for weekday evenings. What are some of your ideas or thoughts on how we can this together?"

Isn't this exciting? Your inner Queen is rising, and she's walking with grace, wisdom, and power.

As we move forward, you'll meet several relationship personality types and the common emotional missteps each one tends to make. And if we're being honest, you may recognize pieces of yourself in more than one of them—I certainly did.

That's okay. It's all part of the growth process. Each revelation is another key to unlocking love that is healthy, whole, and heaven-sent.

Are you ready to tap into your next hidden superpower?

In the next chapter, *"The Kingmaker vs. The Man Breaker,"* we'll explore the incredible influence a woman carries in a relationship. You'll discover just how powerful a Queen truly is, not only in the heart of her kingdom, but in the strength and rise of her King.

Ready for your next milestone in the soulmate journey? Let's go!

Practical Application

"How Do You Really Communicate in Love?" Mini Quiz

Let's take a fun and eye-opening quiz to reflect on how you tend to respond in real-life relationship moments. Remember, awareness and personal responsibility are the first steps to healing and creating different results in love.

For the full deep-dive version (with a strategy guide sent to your inbox), head over to:

www.thesoulmatestrategist.com

Let's get started!

Mini Quiz

Find out which communication patterns may be blocking connection, and what you can do to grow.

Instructions:

Answer each question honestly. Circle the letter that most closely matches your typical response.

1. When you feel hurt or misunderstood by a man, what do you usually say first?

A.) "You never listen to me!"

B.) "I feel hurt and need to talk this through."

C.) "You always make everything about you!"

D.) I shut down and avoid it altogether.

2. When he shares an idea you disagree with, how do you respond?

A.) "That's ridiculous."

B.) "I see your point, but here's my take..."

C.) "Why would you even think that?"

D.) I interrupt and offer a better solution.

3. When you're frustrated during a disagreement, what do you tend to do?

A.) "Whatever."

B.) "Let's take a break and revisit this later."

C.) "I'm done talking to you."

D.) I get sarcastic or start raising my voice.

4. Do you use absolutes like *"always"* or *"never"* during conflict?

      A.) Yes, especially when I'm emotional.

      B.) Rarely, I focus on the current issue.

      C.) Only when I feel really hurt.

      D.) Often, without realizing it.

5. When something's wrong, how do you bring it up?

      A.) I unload everything at once.

      B.) I wait until we're both calm, then speak gently.

      C.) I let it build until I explode.

      D.) I guilt trip or withhold love.

6. How do you respond when he needs space or time alone?

      A.) "Why are you ignoring me again?"

      B.) "Take your time, I'm here when you're ready to talk."

      C.) "Wow, guess you don't care about me at all."

      D.) I pretend I'm fine but give the cold shoulder.

7. When your expectations aren't met (like no call or late reply), you usually.

      A.) Send a passive-aggressive text or stop responding altogether.

      B.) Clarify expectations kindly next time:

        "Hey, I really appreciate it when you check in."

C.) Confront him immediately:

"I can't believe you forgot again!"

D.) Assume the worst, internalize it, and spiral emotionally.

Answer Key & Insights

Total your answers and count how many you selected for each letter:

A's: _____   **B's:** _____   **C's:** _____   **D's:** _____

Mostly A's – The Volcano (Needs Regulation & Reframe)

You have big feelings, and they are valid! But when they erupt unfiltered, they can damage trust. Phrases like *"You always"* or *"Whatever!"* cause defensiveness and disconnection. Practice pausing, breathing, and replacing blame with feelings: *"I feel"* vs. *"You always."*

Growth Tip:

Journal before speaking. Try saying:

"What I'm really needing is…" or

"Can we talk about what just happened?"

Mostly B's – The Conscious Communicator (Strong *EQ!*)

You're intentional and mindful with your words. You've cultivated emotional maturity, and it shows. Your communication builds trust and safety.

Growth Tip:

Stay consistent even when emotions run high. Emotional intelligence is a skill that requires muscle memory. You're doing

Stay consistent even when emotions run high. Emotional intelligence is a skill that requires muscle memory. You're doing great!

Mostly C's – The Critical Controller (Needs Softening & Support)

You often speak from a place of fear or hurt, which can come across as judgmental or harsh. You may not intend to criticize, but it lands that way.

Growth Tip:

Replace loaded phrases like *"What's wrong with you?"* with something like *"Help me understand what you meant."*

Mostly D's – The Shutdown Queen (Needs Vulnerability & Voice)

You may withdraw to protect your heart, but emotional avoidance creates distance.

When you internalize pain, it leaves room for misunderstanding.

Growth Tip:

Practice small expressions of truth. Try a voice note, text, or journal entry when face-to-face sharing feels hard.

Practical Exercise:

From Code to Clarity, Communication Reframing

These exercises are designed to help you grow in emotional intelligence by learning how to express your needs with clarity, confidence, and kindness.

Instructions:

Identify 1–3 situations where you used *"code speak"* instead of directly expressing your feelings or needs.

(Examples include hinting, sulking, sarcasm, or assuming he should *"just know"*.)

For each situation, write down:

- What you said.
- What you actually meant.
- How the situation could have gone differently with clearer communication.

Now reframe your original words into a direct, emotionally intelligent statement.

Example:

Code Speak:

"Boy, there's a lot of work to be done."

Clear Speak:

"I'm feeling overwhelmed and would really appreciate your help with this."

Practice rewriting your own examples in your journal or with a trusted friend.

Remember:

Speaking your truth with kindness is one of the most powerful tools you can develop.

It builds connection, respect, and emotional safety.

Congratulations, beautiful!

You're doing a fabulous job leaning in, showing up, and pressing forward in your growth!

Don't forget to share your reflections or aha moments in the FB Solo to Soulmate Sisterhood Group, we'd love to celebrate with you.

Feeling Ambitious? Try These Optional Journal Reflections:

- In past relationships, where did I react instead of respond?
- How might using inquisitive, non-accusatory language have shifted the outcome?
- Which new phrase or tone shift do I want to practice this week?
- How has my understanding of emotional intelligence changed after this chapter?
- Where do I sense God gently inviting me to grow stronger emotionally?

Optional Prayer:

Father, teach me emotional wisdom. Help me to pause before reacting and speak truth in love. Heal the wounded places within me, and make me a woman of grace, strength, and dignity. In Jesus' name, Amen.

Heart Reflections
FROM JOANNA

Way to go, beautiful!

You just unlocked one of the most powerful foundations for relationship success: **emotional intelligence.**

If you ever feel triggered or overwhelmed, give yourself permission to pause. Take a walk, breathe, and return with a clear heart. One step at a time.

You've learned the difference between reacting and responding. You've discovered the strength of asking with curiosity instead of accusation.

Now pause with me…Place your hand over your heart and acknowledge this truth: **You're growing. You're healing. You're breaking generational cycles.**

Pretty powerful, isn't it?

You've now mastered **three foundational pillars**:
• Recognizing selfish motives (The WIIFM Syndrome)
• Healing your inner mirror (identity and self-worth)
• Strengthening your emotional intelligence and communication

Next, we're stepping into a superpower most women don't even realize they hold: **the power of a Queen—to build a man up as a Kingmaker or tear him down as a Man-Breaker.**

Understanding this will radically shift how you attract and sustain a healthy, God-aligned love story.

Are you ready? Here we go!

Chapter Five

THE KINGMAKER VS. THE MAN BREAKER

> *WOMEN MARRY MEN HOPING THEY WILL CHANGE.*
> *MEN MARRY WOMEN HOPING THEY WILL NOT.*
> *EACH IS INEVITABLY DISAPPOINTED.*
> ALBERT EINSTEIN

Aren't we often waiting for the *perfect* man to come along? Then if he shows up, don't we often slide into the role of helper, fixer, or coach?

We see potential. We mean well. We have vision. We can change him.

After all, we women often believe we know best, right?

But here's the raw, and powerful truth: YOU CAN NEVER CHANGE A MAN.

No matter how well-intentioned you are, nothing will push a good man away faster than:

- Making him feel like he's not good enough.
- Trying to change or *"improve"* him.
- Redoing his efforts (translation: telling him he did it wrong).
- Dismissing his compliments or acts of love.
- Constantly one-upping or correcting him.

When this happens, here's how he feels: Rejected. Defeated. Discouraged.

And his internal dialogue becomes: *"Why bother trying if nothing I do is ever enough?"*

A Queen's True Power

In the game of chess, the queen is the most powerful piece on the board. She can take out opponents, protect the king, and move with grace and strength in every direction.

She has power, and how she wields that power can change the fate of the entire kingdom (the king). Beautiful, you are that queen.

When I began studying women who had the kind of thriving, joyful, God-centered marriages I desired, I noticed something stunning. These women shared a pattern, an energy, a presence that I now call *"The Kingmaker Spirit."*

These women:

- Carried inner confidence, not performance.
- Genuinely enjoyed men instead of fearing or resenting them.
- Set healthy boundaries with grace, not control.
- Honored their men, both publicly and privately.

They were Kingmakers. They didn't just see their man's flaws; they saw his future. They called it forth.

Quick note: I'm not talking about taking on man-projects (we'll cover that in a later chapter). I'm talking about drawing out the king.

What does a kingmaker do?

A. She reflects the superhero man mirror.
B. She publicly and privately affirms him.
C. She doesn't accuse but inquires inquisitively.

In fact, the Kingmaker calls out the superhero qualities within him, the protector, the provider, the strength. She sees who he is (and who he is growing into) and speaks to that. We discussed these foundation stones of superhero deactivator behaviors in Chapter Two.

Again...I'm not talking about adopting a man-project... more to come on that!

The Man-Breaker: Death by a Thousand Cuts

While a Kingmaker calls out the best in a man, a Man-Breaker often unintentionally tears him down.

She shames, belittles, and emasculates, sometimes without even realizing it. But to a man, it can feel like death by a thousand cuts, tiny, wounding words from the woman he loves and wants to impress.

This pain is often delivered in subtle but consistent ways:

- Criticizing instead of appreciating.
- Correcting instead of celebrating.
- Shaming instead of shielding.

These reactions are rarely about him. More often, they stem from unhealed wounds in the woman's heart:

- Childhood trauma or neglect.
- Betrayal or heartbreak in a previous relationship.
- Fear of being vulnerable again.
- Deep-rooted insecurity or not feeling *"enough."*
- A need to control and direct.

These heart wounds can become like tangled vines, choking out the life of even the healthiest love.

We can't heal by punishing the next man for what the last man did.

When man-breaking behaviors go unchecked, they don't just damage a relationship, they can scar a man's heart.

Even an emotionally available, godly man can start to retreat, question himself, or shut down emotionally.

Sometimes, the damage is so deep, the next woman he meets has to help him heal, if he's even willing to love again.

Your Words Carry Life or Death

Scripture tells us, *"The tongue has the power of life and death"* (Proverbs 18:21, NIV).

We can't change other people, but we *can* change how we show up and shift our own behaviors, attitudes, and responses. We can become the thermostats in our relationships—setting the emotional temperature with grace, empathy, and wisdom.

You wouldn't want another woman wounding your Mr. Potential before he ever finds you right?

And you certainly don't want to be *that* woman either.

You are learning to walk like a Queen—strong, radiant, emotionally wise. Together, we are becoming Kingmakers... not Man-Breakers.

As you grow in emotional wisdom, you'll begin to notice something beautiful: **the healthier you become, the healthier the men you attract.**

Your inner transformation becomes a magnet for God-aligned love you desire.

> *YOU MUST BE THE CHANGE YOU WISH TO SEE IN*
> *THE WORLD.*
> GANDHI

In the **WIIFM** Syndrome chapter, we talked about how media and cultural programming shape our beliefs around love, relationships, and stereotypes of men and women.

Subtle cultural shaming can sneak in without our awareness.

For example: How often have you heard phrases like, *"Happy wife, happy life."?*

We laugh at these sayings.

They've become socially accepted punchlines.

But let's pause and unpack them.

What are they really saying?

The underlying message is this: The husband's needs don't matter. His voice isn't important. It's all about the woman. He's just doing it.

Remember the latest version of the Barbie movie's theme? Barbie lived in full color. Ken only existed in shades of grey.

Do you see how insidious this programming can be, and we don't realize it?

So instead of saying, *"Happy wife, happy life,"* how about we choose, **"Happy spouse, happy house"?**

Because in a healthy, loving relationship, both hearts matter.

Marriage is a partnership, not a one-sided performance.

Examples of the Man-Breaker

Let's take a deeper look at a specific form of man-breaking behavior, *"The Shamer."*

The Shamer disrespects, belittles, or publicly and privately embarrasses her man. She makes him feel inadequate, not because he is, but because she is operating out of fear, control, or deep insecurity.

Controlling behaviors are almost always rooted in fear and unresolved pain.

The Shamer rarely expresses gratitude for the things her man does. She overlooks the thoughtful gestures, both big and small. She talks over him, interrupts him, and makes her irritation about what he did, or didn't do, loud and obvious to everyone within earshot.

She may dismiss his efforts, downplay his work, or disregard the time and energy he's poured into doing something for her, all because she's carrying an entitlement mindset or the *"What's In It For Me?"* **(WIIFM) Syndrome**. At the root of these behaviors? Unforgiveness. Bitterness. A need for control.

These negative attitudes are like weeds in a garden.

And what do weeds do? They start small, take root quietly, and eventually spread under the surface until they choke out the life of every healthy plant around them.

I've seen it too often, women who carry unhealed pain from childhood abuse or betrayal in past relationships. Some refuse to deal with it. Others bury it. But over time, buried pain resurfaces as sharp words, judgment, and emotional walls.

Sometimes, the pain from one man is taken out on another, especially on a good man.

It becomes a silent but dangerous cycle: *"You hurt me in the past, and I won't let it go. Therefore, you owe me. I'm going to make sure you pay for it, repeatedly."*

Unforgiveness says: *"You owe me."*

Bitterness says: *"I'll never let you forget it."*

Revenge says: *"I'll make you regret it."*

These are the silent killers of connection.

Let's be real. Bitterness and unforgiveness don't just damage relationships — they age your soul. They drain your joy. And they blind you to the good in a man who may be trying his best to love you well.

I've been there. (You remember the Pillsbury Doughboy moment.) If you've caught yourself doing this, you're not alone.

And if you're thinking, *"Oh wow, I know someone who does this,"* don't be surprised. Many of us picked up shaming behaviors without even realizing it.

But now it's time to shift — to choose awareness, healing, and a healthier way to love.

Let's look at some more real-life examples of The Shamer, some subtle, some extreme, so we can begin to recognize and uproot these behaviors.

The Conference Speaker Shamer

I once watched a well-known speaker publicly humiliate her husband, multiple times in a single evening.

First, from the stage, she laughed and said, *"Don't mind him behind my book table, he's just the wallpaper!"*

The audience winced. The laughter was nervous, not warm.

Later, at the book table, her husband accidentally handed a customer the wrong book.

She snapped, *"Can't you do anything right?!"*

His face fell. The shame was palpable. The customer quickly walked away, uncomfortable and disheartened.

This woman thought she was being witty. She thought she was owning the room like a confident queen. But to everyone watching, she looked more like a mean-spirited tyrant in a microphone and high heels.

Remember, little keys unlock big doors. Big doors swing on small hinges.

Publicly honor your man. Privately correct with grace. Because even a subtle put-down, is still a put-down.

Have you ever witnessed a woman who makes fun of her man in front of others?

Or maybe she jokingly complains about all the things her husband isn't, not smart enough, not handy enough, not ambitious enough?

Have you ever been around a woman with a demeaning attitude toward her guy?

Are these Kingmaker behaviors? Or are they Superhero Deactivators?

The Self-Justified Shamer

Let me introduce you to Tami.

Tami had been married to Robert for 28 years. But instead of choosing to heal the deep wounds from her childhood abuse and betrayal from a previous marriage, she carried those wounds into her current relationship, unprocessed and unresolved.

Rather than seeking healing, Tami unknowingly weaponized her pain against Robert through years of:

- Constant shaming.
- Passive-aggressive nagging.
- Harsh accusations.
- Public and private humiliation.
- Holding old mistakes over his head for decades.

And here's the heartbreaking part.

Even after Robert apologized deeply and repeatedly and genuinely worked to change the mistakes of his past, Tami refused to let it go.

Bitterness became her baseline. Control became her comfort zone. Love could no longer breathe in that space.

One day, Tami pulled me aside and asked, *"How do I get Robert to change his behavior? He constantly irritates me, and he lies about finishing things when he hasn't."*

I paused, then asked gently, *"Are you sure you want the truth?"*

She nodded, so I spoke truth, with kindness and courage.

"Tami, what if you started affirming Robert instead of shaming him? What if you celebrated what he's doing right instead of only pointing out what's wrong?"

Her reaction?

She was furious.

She stopped speaking to me.

Sadly, she refused to change.

Instead, she doubled down on her frustration, digging in her heels with even more nastiness and blame.

Pain that is not healed becomes poison. Bitterness is not a strength; it's like rotting wood to the soul. Shame never transforms a heart; it only shuts it down.

You were made to breathe life, not choke it out with criticism.

You are called to be a Kingmaker, not a Man-Breaker.

Even the smallest choice to speak life instead of shame can unlock a brand-new door in your relationship.

> **BETTER TO DWELL IN THE WILDERNESS, THAN WITH A CONTENTIOUS (LIKELY TO CAUSE DISAGREEMENT OR ARGUMENT) AND ANGRY WOMAN.**
>
> JOANNA'S INTERPRETATION OF PROVERBS 21:19, KJV

Unfortunately, and unexpectedly, Tami passed away in her sleep, still trapped in her bitterness.

And Robert?

After her death, he blossomed.

The heavy atmosphere of constant shaming, accusations, belittling lifted, and for the first time in years, he began to smile, to laugh, to live again.

Let that sink in.

What could a man become if he no longer lived under the weight of criticism?

Food for Thought as We Forge Ahead

Take a moment to reflect on these questions:

- Do you have unresolved feelings from a past relationship?
- Are you still holding on to unhealed anger or resentment toward men?
- Do you always feel the need to argue a point?
- Do you always have to be right?
- Do you have to have the last word?
- Do you feel the need to control a relationship? And deep down, are you afraid of getting hurt?

These questions aren't meant to shame or condemn you.

They're an invitation to freedom. To healing. To love that lasts.

The Subtle Shamer

My friend Mike once dated a woman he really liked. One day, he showed her a picture of his dear friend Don, a man who had endured years of bullying due to obesity and a rare skin condition.

Without thinking, she blurted out: *"Eww! Who is that? He looks weird and ugly."*

Mike stared at her in shock. He had been seriously considering proposing to her.

But in that moment, he realized something important: Her heart wasn't beautiful. And just like that, the relationship ended.

What could she have done differently?

If she had concerns or questions, she could have responded with compassion:

"Tell me about Don. What's his story?"

That simple shift would have revealed empathy and kindness, not cruelty.

A Man Values Your Voice

Never forget this, beautiful one: **a man values his woman's voice more than anyone else's.**

Your future Mr. Right — or your current Mr. Potential — hears your words louder than the world around him.

When you belittle, correct, or dismiss him, you're not just hurting his feelings. You're chiseling away at the foundation of love, trust, and emotional safety.

Each time sarcasm, contempt, or harshness slips in, it becomes a quiet wound — a cut to the heart of a man who wants to love you well.

As my husband once said, *"When a man's queen shames him, it feels like he's being stabbed in the heart."*

But when you build him up:

When you speak life, appreciation, and belief into him…you awaken his inner superhero.

You become the living, breathing Man Mirror that reflects his strength back to him.

This is what a Queen does. And this is who you are becoming.

So, take heart, trailblazer. None of us gets this perfectly.

We're all learning. We're all growing.

But you — yes, *you* — are rising higher than most women because you're choosing awareness over autopilot, healing over hiding, and love over fear.

The love of God covers you, heals you, and empowers every step of your journey.

And the most incredible part?

You are beginning to shift everything!

Now… let's sail into the next chapter.
Are you ready to discover how a woman can unintentionally train a man *not* to compliment her, *not* to bring flowers, *not* to help, and *not* to pursue?

Ready? Let's go.

Practical Application

Let's put some of this heart work into action. Real growth happens when insight meets intention. Here are a few soul nourishing steps to help you shift from man-breaking patterns to queen-building power:

Use your words to give life.

Be intentional with your language. Speak words that build up, not tear down. Life and death are in the power of the tongue (Proverbs 18:21). Use yours to speak life over the men in your life, and yourself.

Become aware of cultural *"man jabs."*

Start noticing the subtle, often *"joking"* putdowns about men that are embedded in our culture. Make it a habit to find something good to compliment, even in small things. A grateful heart trains your eyes to see differently.

Be willing to say, *"I'm sorry."*

As you reflect on this chapter, you might realize you've engaged in some behaviors you're not proud of.

That's okay. Give yourself grace. But also be brave enough to explore the root behind them, fear, insecurity, or unhealed wounds, and bring those places before God.

Make amends where appropriate.

If you feel led, and it's safe and healthy to do so, go back and apologize to the person you may have hurt. Take responsibility. Affirm what they did right.

If direct conversation isn't possible, try this:

Write a letter you don't send. Pour your heart out. Forgive. Let go.

You'll be amazed at how liberating it feels.

Identify and uproot man-breaking patterns.

Take time to list past behaviors that may have chipped away at your relationships. Then, beside each one, write what you believe was the deeper root, a fear of abandonment, past betrayal, need for control, or something else.

Awareness is the first step to transformation. Write down what things you've become aware of.

_____

_____

_____

_____

_____

_____

_____

_____

_____

_____

_____

_____

Heart Reflections
FROM JOANNA

Great job, Queen!

What stood out to you?
Every mindset shift and *"aha"* moment brings more freedom. Truth doesn't just convict — it liberates.

Take a moment to celebrate your progress. And if you're feeling bold, share a win in the Solo to Soulmate Sisterhood FB group. We're cheering you on.

Your Kingmaker Action Steps:

• **Celebrate First:** Notice what he does right — even the small things — and thank him sincerely.
• **Pause Before You Speak:** Ask yourself, *"Will these words build him up or tear him down?"*
• **Forgive the Past:** If he's growing, don't drag old mistakes into today. Love thrives in grace.
• **Pray for Fresh Eyes:** Ask God to help you see your man or future man the way Heaven sees him.

And beautiful Queen… you're doing it.

In the next chapter, we're going to uncover a surprising personality trait that can quietly shut down passion, connection, and pursuit — even with a good man.

More importantly, you'll learn exactly how to shift it.

Smile, breathe, and grab your journal. Ready for your next breakthrough?

Chapter Six

THE REVERSE TRAINER

*I CAN LIVE FOR TWO MONTHS ON
A GOOD COMPLIMENT.*
MARK TWAIN

Everyone appreciates a sincere compliment. But how many of us truly know how to receive one without brushing it off, deflecting it, or feeling like we must immediately bounce it back like a tennis ball?

Let's pause and be clear: I'm not talking about flattery, that's insincere praise, often used to manipulate. I'm talking about a real, heartfelt compliment. A simple, *"You look radiant today,"* or *"You did a great job on that project."*

Can you receive that kind of truth with open hands and a soft heart?

Although my personal journey through singleness was long and full of unexpected detours, it became the best education I could have asked for.

Every revelation, every course correction along the way brought me to this moment, sharing these golden keys with you.
And one of those keys might surprise you.

Did you know? Rejecting a compliment is a form of reverse training.

You might be thinking, *"Reverse training? What in the world is that?"*

I'm so glad you asked. Grab your tea (or coffee), and let's cozy in for this heart-to-heart.

What Is a Reverse Trainer?

When your inability to receive outweighs your capacity to give, you unintentionally become what I call a Reverse Trainer.

This term was first shared with me by an incredible business coach. I never forgot her words, *"Joanna, we teach people how to treat us."*

Here's what it means in practice:

- A Reverse Trainer unconsciously teaches others to stop giving to her.
- She unintentionally draws negative attention to herself.
- She blocks blessings, not just from people, but also from God.
- She makes others feel foolish, dismissed, or rejected when they try to love her or compliment her.

And the saddest part? She often doesn't even realize she's doing it.

One of the most significant areas where women struggle with reverse training is in the art of receiving, especially compliments or gifts.

So many women (me included, back in the day) find it difficult to simply accept kind words or gestures without minimizing, deflecting, or feeling obligated to give something back.

Here's the deeper truth:

Every woman carries some form of insecurity, whether it's about her body, her worth, her voice, or her place in the world. It could be her weight, height, hair, skin tone, or body shape. For others, it might be not feeling smart enough, pretty enough, worthy enough, capable enough, or even spiritual enough.

When those insecurities mix with subconscious shame or self-rejection, it creates a dangerous block to receiving. We may fall into patterns of passive-aggressive behavior, *"code speak,"* or the victim mindset. We become over-givers while denying ourselves the beauty of receiving love in return.

Quick Self-Check (Be Honest, Beautiful Queen!)

Ask yourself:

- Do you struggle to accept compliments without brushing them off?
- Do you feel compelled to return a compliment immediately, like a transaction?
- Does receiving a gift make you feel uncomfortable or obligated to *"pay it back"*?
- Is your identity wrapped in being the Rescuer, the Fixer, or the Martyr?
- When someone says, *"You're beautiful,"* do you inwardly cringe or think, *"Yeah, right"*?

If you answered *yes* to any of those questions, you are not alone.

I've been there. So have thousands of women I've worked with.

The good news?

Awareness is the beginning of breakthrough. And you, beautiful, are already on your way.

A Gentle Wake-Up Call

One day, while meditating on why certain blessings in my life felt *"stuck,"* I had a vivid vision. In it, I offered a thoughtful, beautiful bouquet of flowers to a dear friend.

She looked at them, sneered, and slapped me in the face with the bouquet. Petals flew everywhere. I stood there, stunned, first angry, then rejected, and finally, deeply hurt.

Then I heard the Holy Spirit whisper,

"This is how you make people feel when you reject their compliments. You slap away their gifts. You reject My blessings. You reject them. You leave them feeling, rejected, sad and angry"

Wow. What a wake-up call!

Right then and there, I made a decision:

I would become a woman who receives well, with grace, gratitude, and joy.

What Men Experience When You Reject Their Gifts
(Compliments, Thoughtful Acts, Kind Gestures)

Later, my perspective deepened even more through a conversation with my husband, David. He told me that during his single years, it was *rare* for women to receive his compliments sincerely.

He said it was frustrating, exhausting, even.

He wasn't trying to flatter or manipulate anyone.

He was offering genuine admiration.

But time and again, women dismissed the compliment. Their inability to simply receive it made him feel drained, disconnected, and eventually disinterested.

Beloved, does this sound familiar?

Let me share one of my own hard-earned lessons.

At a social gathering, I found myself in a great conversation with a kind, great guy. The exchange flowed easily, until he complimented me on my outfit.

I was feeling bloated that day, and instead of receiving it, I blurted out,

"Oh, you're just saying that. Look how bloated my stomach is, and this outfit is old."

The look on his face said it all.

He stared at me, unsure of what to say. He had been sincere, and I had just called him a liar, rejected his kindness, and criticized myself all in one breath.

He politely excused himself, and I was left wondering why he didn't ask for my number.

Looking back, I now clearly see the superhero deactivators at play in that one moment:

- I called him a liar. I rejected his gift (the compliment).
- I drew negative attention to my body (which he hadn't even noticed).
- I insulted myself as a poor dresser.

I was the Reverse Trainer. What do you think my romance results where? Dateless.

A good Mr. Potential was repelled, and it essentially set the stage for Mr. Wrong to come along and mistreat me.

Now imagine the opposite scenario. What if I had smiled and said,

"Thank you so much! I receive that."

And meant it?

He probably would have asked me out. He would've felt honored, appreciated, and encouraged.

A sincere compliment lands when it's graciously received.

A Simple Shift with Big Impact

When your man compliments you and you dismiss or question it, why would he keep trying?

You've unknowingly activated a **superhero deactivator** and trained him not to bother.

Does this behavior draw him closer... or quietly push him away?

Now imagine how he (or your future man) might feel when you:

- Smile with genuine appreciation
- Say warmly, *"Thank you, I receive that!"*
- Light up the moment with your gratitude.

You create a safe space for his masculinity to shine. You make him want to give again.

He'll bring flowers, plan surprises, offer kind gestures, because you make him feel seen, honored, and valued.

Receiving well is a SUPERPOWER.

What's our mantra beautiful queen? Little keys unlock big doors. Big doors swing on small hinges.

> ***FREELY YOU HAVE RECEIVED; FREELY GIVE.***
> MATTHEW 10:8B (NIV)

Receiving with grace might feel small, but it can open doors to love you never imagined.

Let's Look at Some Common Reverse Training Scenarios:

Scenario	Reverse Trainer Response	Hidden Message
Friend says: *"Your outfit looks great!"*	*"Oh, this old thing?"*	*"You're wrong. I don't believe you."*
Boyfriend says: *"You're amazing."*	*"You're just saying that."*	*"I don't trust you or your words."*
Husband brings flowers	*"Why waste money on flowers?"*	*"I'm not worth small gestures of love."*
Husband gives lingerie gift	*"All you want is sex!"*	*"Your desire for me is wrong and dirty. I don't want you to want me."*

Each time you reject the gift, you shrink the connection.

Each time you receive with honor, you build a bridge of trust.

Receiving well is a queenly skill.

Here's a simple, powerful strategy to practice:

1. Smile warmly.

2. Look the giver in the eyes.

3. Say with grace: *"Thank you. I receive that."* OR *"How thoughtful, thank you. That really means a lot to me."*

That's it. No need to deflect or explain. No need to return the compliment like a tennis volley. No need to downplay or brush it off. Just receive.

And remember: *Receiving with grace makes others feel good about giving. That's what a Queen does, she receives with dignity, warmth, and power.*

Closing Reflection

You're opening your heart to love, honor, compliments, and blessings — without apology.

You're learning how to be loved well... to allow kindness to land... to receive without shrinking back.

Receiving is giving.

When you receive well, you give others the joy of blessing you. You keep the beautiful cycle of giving and receiving flowing.

Eye-opening, isn't it?

And the best part?
You're changing your story — one courageous choice at a time.

Keep shining, beautiful. You are becoming unstoppable.

Ready for the next chapter?

We're going to uncover a hidden pattern many strong, capable women never realize they're carrying. It's a pattern that quietly erases boundaries, silences needs, and attracts the very men who take advantage of their beautiful hearts.

It's time to meet The Disguised Doormat. And it's time to break free.

Your next goal is to learn how to be a good receiver. And if it feels awkward at first, let's start by giving yourself permission to receive.

Place your hand on your heart (skin to skin if possible) and speak this aloud:

"I give myself permission to receive all the good gifts and blessings Heaven has for me."

Now repeat as needed, slowly, intentionally, with your hand on your heart.

Homework Challenge:

For the next five days, practice being a gracious receiver, without deflecting, minimizing, or feeling obligated to return the gesture.

Examples:

Let's say you are at the store, someone holds a door for you? Smile warmly and say, *"Thank you!"*

Someone gives you a compliment? Look them in the eyes and say, *"Thank you. I receive that."*

Someone blesses you with a gift or kind gesture? Accept it fully, without guilt or explanation.

Journal Reflection:

Each evening, jot down a few thoughts:

- How did it feel to simply receive?
- Was it easy or hard for you?
- Did you catch yourself wanting to downplay, deflect, or *"earn"* the kindness?

What shifted in your spirit as you received with joy?

At one point, all of us have operated in higher or lower degrees of the Reverse Trainer. The key to growth is awareness, intentional practice, and grace.

You're not just doing the work, you're becoming the woman who attracts and sustains heaven-sent love.

I'm so proud of you. Keep going. Keep growing.

Heart Reflections
FROM JOANNA

Wow, beautiful one… what a powerful chapter you just completed.

Take a moment. Breathe deeply… exhale slowly. Feel that? **Freedom.**

You're learning one of the most subtle yet life-changing secrets to love and abundance: **the ability to receive well.**

You discovered that when we reject compliments, kindness, or sincere gestures, we don't just push good men away — we block the flow of love and shut doors we've prayed would open.

But guess what? **You're not that woman anymore.** You're becoming a Queen who smiles, receives, and welcomes love with open arms.

You're retraining your heart, your mind, and your relationships to expect goodness and receive it with joy. That's generational breakthrough.

Beautiful work! Let this be your new daily mantra: **"Thank you. I receive it."**

Whether someone opens a door, carries a bag, or offers a compliment…Smile. Pause. Receive.

Now, are you ready for your next breakthrough?
In the next chapter, we'll explore a sneaky trap many women fall into without realizing it — one that cost me dearly and repelled good men.

But that's about to change for you.

So, take a deep breath. Here we go.

Chapter Seven

THE DISGUISED DOORMAT
(AKA The Yes Syndrome)

> *THE MOST PAINFUL THING IS LOSING YOURSELF IN*
> *THE PROCESS OF LOVING SOMEONE TOO MUCH…*
> *AND FORGETTING THAT YOU ARE SPECIAL, TOO.*
> ERNEST HEMINGWAY

Have you ever lost yourself in a relationship? Have you ever found yourself giving up your power, your preferences, or your identity just to hold on to a man?

If you're nodding your head right now, you're not alone. At one point or another, many of us women have engaged in what I call Disguised Doormat behaviors. (Don't ask me how I know this, let's just say, experience is a thorough teacher.)

As a healthy relationship begins to grow and deepen, it's natural for lives to begin to overlap. You share dreams, calendars, favorite shows, and grocery lists.

When you marry, your lives become intertwined in even greater ways, and that's a beautiful thing.

But what we're about to explore is the unhealthy version of that togetherness.

A pattern of enmeshment that causes a woman to slowly dissolve her identity to keep love.

Who is the Disguised Doormat?

She's strong. She's independent. She's successful in her own right and can confidently stand on her own two feet.

Until she gets into a relationship. Then, something shifts.

She begins to lose her identity, as piece by piece, her thoughts become his thoughts. His hobbies become her hobbies. His social circle replaces hers. His house becomes her whole world.

Have you seen any of your friends or family members go through this?

And underneath it all?

Fear.

It's a fear of losing him. It's a fear of being alone again or a fear of not being enough.

As a result, she gives, and gives, and gives, until she's exhausted, anxious, and resentful.

The Yes Syndrome

The Disguised Doormat becomes the *"Yes, whatever works for you"* woman.

- She says yes to things that violate her values.
- She says yes when she really wants to say no.
- She bends her boundaries, sacrifices her peace, and shrinks herself to keep his affection.

At first, he might enjoy the attention. It can feel flattering.

But what happens over time? He starts to lose respect.

Emotionally healthy men are drawn to women who honor themselves:

- A woman who knows who she is.
- A woman who has her own passions, opinions, and purpose.
- A woman who lives out her God-given identity, regardless of who she's dating or married to.

The more she pleases, the more he pulls away.

And if he's emotionally unhealthy himself? This dynamic can quickly spiral into manipulation, control, or even emotional abuse.

Let's take a deeper look at how this pattern plays out... and most importantly, how to break free.

Because Queen, you were never created to be a doormat. You were designed to be a daughter of the King.

> ### *YOU'LL MISS THE BEST THINGS,*
>
> ### *IF YOU KEEP YOUR EYES SHUT.*
> DR. SEUSS

It usually starts subtly, a slow fade into his world.

- You meet someone who seems wonderful.
- You laugh. You flirt. You feel alive.
- You start doing things he enjoys, spending more time at his place, choosing his favorite restaurants.

And before you even realize it, your friends become a faint echo, your hobbies collect dust, and the vibrant woman he was first drawn to has quietly vanished.

It's subtle, like being swept away in a gentle tide you didn't notice rising.

Somewhere in your beautiful desire to love well, you forget how to love wisely.

You become the *"yes"* girl who is:

Always available. Always agreeable. Always over-giving.

Always shrinking to fit his schedule, his mood, his needs.

Until one day, you're no longer standing beside him as an equal, but lying beneath him like a rug.

He starts to lose interest. He begins to pull away. And the more he distances himself, the more desperately you try to grasp for his attention, his affection, his presence.

How many times have you watched this happen to your friends?

Has it happened to you?

The Pilot Who Flew Away

Before I married Mr. Wrong, I dated a great Mr. Potential.

He was a handsome pilot with a magnetic smile and a gift for sweeping gestures.

In the beginning, I was confident, independent, full of joy and sparkle.

He was spontaneous and romantic. He made me feel cherished and seen.

It felt like a fairytale.

Once, he rolled out a literal red carpet sprinkled with rose petals, leading to a private Cessna plane, just to fly me to dinner in another city.

Another time, he surprised me on the 4th of July with a night flight, soaring above fireworks sparkling across the skyline.

He played the piano. He serenaded me for my birthday. He made me feel like the only woman on earth.

And then, I slowly disappeared.

I stopped going out with my friends.

I gave up my routines.

I became his *"yes woman,"* scheduling my life around his preferences, his timing, and his desires.

The more available I became, the less available he was.

The more I tried to win his attention, the more he pulled back.

And the more he withdrew, the more I found myself anxiously asking, *"Are you upset with me?"*, not to manipulate, but to soothe the deep fear I didn't want to admit was there.

Here's what I didn't understand at the time:

What makes a diamond valuable isn't just its beauty, it is the rarity.

A diamond isn't begging to be noticed. It stands in its brilliance.

It doesn't chase; it shines.

Without realizing it, I had become the Disguised Doormat, a woman cloaked in affection that was really rooted in fear and lack of self-worth.

What Makes a Woman Magnetic?

It's not perfection that makes a woman magnetic; it's her presence.

Men are drawn to women who smile with joy, walk in quiet confidence, and live with purpose.

- A woman who honors her time, her voice, her values.
- A woman who sets boundaries without apology.
- A woman who respects herself and invites others to do the same.

She radiates peace. She radiates strength.

And in doing so, she naturally attracts a man who recognizes her worth, not because she fights for it, but because she walks in it. A woman with a radiant smile can outshine anyone in the room.

Healthy men are not attracted to women who pursue them or reshape their entire world around them. That kind of over-giving repels good men and potentially attracts abusers or narcissists.

The more a woman erases her own life to be consumed by his, the more she risks being overlooked, or taken for granted.

A woman who's constantly asking where he is, what he's thinking, or fearing abandonment doesn't communicate confidence, she communicates anxiety. And anxiety is rooted in fear, not attraction.

Emotionally mature men are drawn to women who have a voice, who aren't afraid to express a different opinion or lovingly call them out when needed. They don't just tolerate that, they respect it.

What Does a Disguised Doormat Look Like in Real Life?

- She cancels girls' nights just in case he might want to hang out.
- She's strong and self-sufficient, until she's emotionally entangled.
- She's successful and independent, until his opinion becomes the most important one, in an unhealthy way.

- She says *"yes"* to things she dislikes, just to avoid conflict or the fear he might leave.
- She waits anxiously for his texts, rearranges her life for him, and panics when he goes quiet.
- She apologizes even when she hasn't done anything wrong.
- She seeks his approval like a lifeline. As she fades, so does his respect.

The Story of Cheryl

Cheryl was a gifted therapist with a vibrant social life and a heart full of joy. She married a charming, funny, and successful man. At first, their chemistry sizzled. But after marriage, Cheryl slowly slipped into the "Yes Syndrome."

Her world began shrinking to fit his.

She stopped seeing friends.

She stopped doing the things that made her come alive.

The confident, dynamic woman he fell in love with, became a shell, an agreeable shadow, trying to keep peace and avoid conflict.

He began to test her boundaries: Sly remarks. Subtle put downs. Probing to see if she'd push back. She didn't.

The disrespect escalated constant criticism, nothing she did was good enough. Then came the affairs.

And still, Cheryl tried harder to please him.

The more she coddled him, the more contempt he showed her.

The more she appeased, the more boldly he betrayed.

This wasn't Cheryl's first heartbreak. It was her second marriage, and her second pattern of disappearing.

The Emotional Payoff of Being a Doormat

Is there a hidden *"payoff"* to being a disguised doormat?

Sometimes, we unconsciously wear our martyrdom like a badge of honor.

We tell others how mistreated we are, hoping for sympathy.

We post vague or sad messages, longing for someone to check in or feel sorry for us.

We trade self-abandonment for emotional currency.

Other times, being the doormat is a twisted way to seek attention.

She allows the guy to disrespect her. She doesn't set boundaries. She silently hopes he'll see her sacrifices and change.

But here's the truth:

Enabling bad behavior doesn't heal it. Avoiding conflict doesn't earn respect.

Shrinking yourself doesn't make someone love you more.

A woman with a radiant smile can outshine anyone in the room.

Healthy men are not attracted to women who pursue them or reshape their entire world around them. *That kind of over-giving repels good men.* The more a woman erases her own life to be consumed by his, the more she risks being overlooked, or taken for granted.

A woman who's constantly asking where he is, what he's thinking, or fearing abandonment doesn't communicate

116

confidence, she communicates anxiety. And anxiety is rooted in fear, not attraction.

Emotionally mature men are drawn to women who have a voice, who aren't afraid to express a different opinion or lovingly call them out when needed. They don't just tolerate that, they respect it.

> *NO ONE CAN MAKE YOU FEEL INFERIOR WITHOUT YOUR CONSENT.*
>
> ELEANOR ROOSEVELT

Remember, we teach people how to treat us.

I once had a boss who publicly demeaned me, pointed out my mistakes in meetings, and spoke down to me with constant condescending tones.

I'd cry while driving home every week. People felt sorry for me and would affirm me with phrases such as, *"He's so awful to you." "You're such a good person; you don't deserve that." "I can't believe how he treats you." "You should get a medal of honor for having to work with him."* The co-workers showered me with attention.

But one day, a brave coworker looked me in the eye and asked,

"Joanna, do you know people are calling you a doormat behind your back?"

I stared at her, stunned and speechless.

Then she leaned in and added gently,

"What do you believe about yourself that allows him to treat you this way?"

OUCH.

That was the truth I didn't want to hear but desperately needed it. And I'm forever grateful she had the courage to speak it.

That moment changed my life.

I began to ask myself: What kind of subconscious emotional payoff was I getting from all this?

In my mind's eye, it was about attention, validation, recognition. I had unknowingly slipped into passive-aggressive behavior. He looked like the bad guy and I looked like the innocent victim.

But once I recognized that pattern, I made a decision and took responsibility for my choices.

I enrolled in courses to learn healthy relationship skills.

I worked through my fears and approval issues.

I studied how to hold crucial conversations and respectfully confront behavior without being passive-aggressive, or a *"snitch."*

And guess what?

I finally stood up to my boss. Calmly. Clearly. Firmly.

And I didn't allow him to mistreat me again.

FREEDOM.

A woman who truly knows her worth stands out like a diamond to a good man.

Jane's Reset

Jane was married with children and a full plate of responsibilities.

But something had shifted. Her husband had grown distant.

She tried to bridge the gap, planning date nights, suggesting family outings, checking in constantly.

Are you okay? Are you mad at me? What are you thinking?

The more she pursued him, the more irritable, withdrawn, and critical he became.

Finally, on New Year's Eve, Jane hit her limit.

She packed a bag, drove to a friend's house, and left him home alone to stew. There we no texts: No calls. No chasing.

For the first time in a long time, she gave him space.

When she returned the next day, something had shifted.

He apologized. He admitted his behavior. He told her he felt smothered and didn't know how to say it without hurting her.

But here's what changed most:

Jane kept her boundaries.

She started going to the gym again. Reconnected with her friends. Refocused on her passions.

She stopped revolving around him, and he started rotating back toward her.

In a healthy relationship, knowing your worth and walking in it with humble confidence strengthens the foundation of love. But when fear creeps in, it breeds desperation. And desperation is never attractive.

My Wedding Called Off (Then Back On)

After David proposed, we set a wedding date and joyfully began planning, but as his parents' health began to decline, he called me one day and said,

"Joanna, I need to put the wedding on hold. I'm overwhelmed."

The old me would have panicked, spiraling into fear, overthinking, and trying every tactic to keep him from pulling away.

But I didn't. I stayed grounded, calm and secure.

I simply told him I understood and supported him: No drama. No guilt-trips.

Canceling the plans wasn't a problem. I trusted God's timing and took it one step at a time.

Just one week later, he called again:

"Let's move forward. I'm ready."

Why the shift?

Because I didn't lose myself.

I didn't pressure him, try to fix it, or convince him to stay.

I stood in confidence, not fear and that is what drew him closer.

Sometimes, a good man just needs space to process.

As women, we have to learn how to pause without panicking, feeling desperate and how to be still without shrinking.

Ask Yourself:

- Why do I allow his world to consume mine?
- Why do I silence my needs to meet his?

- What am I afraid of losing?
- What attention or emotional payoff am I getting by tolerating mistreatment?

Awareness changes everything.

When you make him your whole world, you both lose.

A healthy man doesn't want a woman who disappears in his shadow.

He wants a woman who knows who she is and invites him to walk beside her.

And beautiful queen, remember:

You can't change anyone, but you can change how *you* respond.

The moment you shift, the energy of the relationship shifts too.

Your confidence becomes the catalyst. Your boundaries become the blessing.

Everything is a choice. The key is being willing to see and take action.

Immediate Actions to Break the Doormat Pattern.

- Reconnect with old friends. Make that call. Book the lunch.
- Reignite your hobbies. Sign up for the class. Take the trip.
- Stop being overly available. Let him miss you.
- Say *no* when needed.
- Take your time back.
- Notice where fear of rejection or abandonment is driving your choices.

- Practice having your own thoughts, boundaries, and opinions, even if he disagrees.
- Start journaling where your sense of identity feels tied to his responses.

You can be a loving, generous woman without being a disappearing one.

As we close this chapter, remember:

Inner confidence is magnetic.

It attracts real, lasting, mutual love, the kind that doesn't demand performance, perfection, or self-erasure. Just your presence.

Coming Up Next...

In the next chapter, we'll meet The Queen of Chaos, a woman whose world is ruled by drama, intensity, and emotional roller coasters that leave love gasping for air.

But first, let's pause for reflection.

Journal Reflections

Mark the statements that resonate. These awareness prompts help you identify old patterns.

- Bad things always happen to me.
- So-and-so made me feel this way.
- There's nothing I can do about it.
- I can't because of _____.
- It's not my fault this keeps happening.
- Nobody cares about me.
- I'm always treated unfairly.
- There's no solution that will help me.
- I'm not comfortable confronting people.

Do you recognize *Yes Syndrome* or victim mindset tendencies in yourself?

If yes, take a few minutes to reflect and pray. Meditate on the moments when you may have unknowingly given your power away.

Victim thinking can be reflected as:

"Things just happen to me. I have no control. Others make me feel this way. I need someone to see and feel sorry for me."

But God didn't create you to live from that place.

Journaling Prompts

- A. What fear or belief causes you to become the man-pleaser in relationships?
- B. When did you first learn that shrinking yourself might help you feel accepted or loved?

Be honest. Be kind to yourself. And remember, you are not the woman you were yesterday. You're rising. You're healing. You're stepping into divine confidence, one page at a time.

_____

_____

_____

_____

_____

What inner beliefs are causing you to get entangled in his world, and lose yourself in the process?

_____

_____

_____

_____

List three things you will do this week to treat yourself with kindness, dignity, and respect.

_____

_____

_____

_____

_____

_____

_____

_____

_____

_____

_____

_____

_____

_____

_____

_____

AFFIRMATIONS

Speak these aloud with energy, intention, and heartfelt emotion.

- I give myself full permission to love and honor myself.
- Saying _"No"_ is an act of self-love, and I give myself permission to say it without guilt.
- I break agreement with the fear of saying No.
- I release the need for approval from others and declare: my own approval is enough.

- I choose to stop rejecting myself and instead, embrace and accept who I am.
- I understand I can't please everyone, and that's okay.
- I am strong, assertive, and true to myself. I am not a people-pleaser, I am a self-respecting, God-honoring woman.
- I attract people who honor my boundaries and value me for who I truly am.
- I welcome healthy love and respectful relationships into my life.
- I hold the power, with God's help, to shift any situation in my life for good.

Speak these daily (as many times as needed), and watch how your mindset begins to shift.

These affirmations retrain your inner dialogue, helping you cultivate healthy boundaries and a renewed sense of self-worth. Over time, you'll notice yourself standing taller, loving stronger, and choosing relationships that reflect the love you're learning to give yourself.

Need a Simple Way to Say *"No"* with Grace?

Try this phrase: *"I would love to help, but I'm not in a position to do that right now."*

It's honest, kind, and honors your limits.

You're doing such powerful work, queen!

I'm so proud of you, keep going! You've got this.

Heart Reflections

FROM JOANNA

Wow, beautiful one… what a powerful chapter you just completed.

Are you beginning to feel more freedom?

You just uncovered one of the most subtle yet life-changing secrets to love: **the ability to receive well.**

When we reject compliments or kindness, we don't just push good men away — we block the flow of love and shut the very doors we've been praying would open.

Let this be your new daily vocabulary: "Thank you. I receive it."

When someone does something nice, opens a door, offers help, or gives a compliment…Smile. Pause. Receive.

You're shifting from rejection to reception… from martyrdom to royalty.

You're retraining your heart to expect goodness — and to receive it with joy.

If you feel led, celebrate your progress in the FB *Solo to Soulmate Sisterhood* group — we'd love to cheer you on.

In the next chapter, we're uncovering a sneaky trap many women fall into without even realizing it — one that cost me dearly and repelled good men.

But that's about to change for you. Let's deep dive into the chapter!

Chapter Eight

THE QUEEN OF CHAOS

> *CHANGE STARTS WITH YOU. BUT IT DOESN'T START UNTIL YOU DO.*
> TOM ZIGLAR

Have you ever felt like your life was spinning in a tornado? Finances flying in one direction, relationships crumbling in another, work stress barreling in from the north, and emotional drama, maybe from an ex or a family member, pirouetting right in the center of it all?

It's like you're spinning and spinning but getting absolutely nowhere. And just when you think you've caught your breath bam! Another storm warning.

I once saw a T-shirt that read: *"Fueled by caffeine and chaos."*

I laughed out loud. Too real, right?

But here's where we get honest: chaos is part of life. We all have seasons where it feels like we're juggling flaming swords while riding a unicycle through a thunderstorm.

The danger comes when chaos becomes a familiar lifestyle, a personality trait, a defining identity.

Tornadoes are unstable, unpredictable, and always dramatic. And if we're not careful, we can become addicted to the thrill of the spin. We get comfortable in the storm. We slap on a crown, sip our triple-shot latte, and unknowingly step into the role of **The Queen of Chaos**.

But here's the twist: when chaos becomes your constant companion, you don't just drain yourself, you unknowingly pull others into your vortex, too.

And often? You secretly hope a good man will ride in and rescue you.

But that's not a relationship, that's a rescue mission.

And Mr. Right isn't signing up to be your emergency response team.

Let's Talk Straight...

One of the biggest early dating mistakes women make is this:

Unleashing the full dump load of chaos on Mr. Potential before the salad even hits the table.

Childhood trauma? Check.

Heart-wrenching breakup stories? Double check.

Financial stress? Triple check.

Family drama that could be a Netflix series? Check, check, and check.

But here's the good news: Chaos doesn't have to define you.

It might be a chapter in your life, but it doesn't have to be the title of your book.

So, take a deep breath. Healing and breakthrough are closer than you think!

The Superman Encounter

At one point in my journey, I worked at a TV production studio. A man who rented one of our editing suites looked like Superman, literally. Shiny black hair, piercing blue eyes, tall, muscular. He was kind, funny, generous, and yes, I had to remind myself to breathe when he walked by.

He dropped subtle hints of interest, and I responded just enough to let him know I was open. Eventually, he asked me out.

The day arrived! Hair done. Nails fresh. Makeup flawless.

New outfit? Secured. I was ready.

Butterflies? Olympic level.

He picked me up and took me to a beautiful, upscale restaurant. The chemistry was crackling. Conversation flowed. Laughter was effortless. I felt safe, seen and comfortable. It felt like I could share anything with him.

And that's when I made the classic **Queen of Chaos** mistake:

I emotionally dumped on Superman.

Somewhere between the appetizer and the entrée, I started spilling out my chaos. I complained about my ex-husband, the heartbreak, betrayals, financial stress, and unresolved trauma.

My intentions were sincere. I was processing my healing journey.

But what I didn't realize was this: he wasn't my therapist. He was just a guy on his first date.

I didn't notice his eyes glancing at his watch, or the polite smile that replaced his sparkle. I just kept unloading my *"emotional storage unit"* onto that white linen tablecloth.

By the time dessert menus arrived, the spark had quietly exited the building.

He politely explained he had an early morning shoot and needed to leave.

Just like that, our fairy tale faded to credits.

Back at work, he remained friendly, kind, professional, but the connection? Gone.

I was confused. Rejected. I couldn't understand what went wrong.

But God, in His grace, had more to show me.

A Full-Circle Moment

A couple of years later, I ran into Superman at a coffee shop. He recognized me instantly, walked over with that same charming smile, and we started catching up.

Then came the moment.

A pause in the conversation, the kind where you can feel truth knocking.

So I practiced courage, took a deep breath and said,

"Can I ask you something?"

He leaned in.

"What made you lose interest after our dinner date?"

He paused, then answered with such gentleness:

"I really liked you. There was a strong spark. But during dinner, I got overwhelmed. You shared so much, your pain, your past, your struggles, and it all came out at once. It was heavy. I didn't

know what to do with all that. It was too much, so I just... backed off. It felt like you still needed to heal."

Ouch.

Yes, it stung, but it also set me free.

I could have spiraled into shame, anger, or embarrassment. But instead, I chose growth.

That conversation helped me see something clearly:

He didn't reject me. He rejected the chaos I was operating in.

This moment always reminds me of one of those classic cartoon scenes, you know.

The one where the character's eyes dart toward the nearest exit while chaos unfolds. If your date looks like he's scanning the room for an escape route, it might not be about him. It might be about the swirling chaos you're unknowingly bringing to the table.

But don't worry, this isn't a chapter of shame. This is a chapter of breakthrough and awareness.

Your crown isn't made of chaos. It's made of clarity.

You're doing great. Let's keep going.

Together, we're unlearning the habits that sabotage connection and stepping into the calm, confident woman you're becoming.

Emotional Dumping = Repelling

When we feel rejected, it's easy to spiral into that old story of *"not enough."*

Not pretty enough. Not skinny enough.

Not smart, funny, spiritual, or successful enough.

But remember this: It was never about enough-ness.

It was about timing and emotional readiness.

I had emotionally flooded him. I'd unknowingly cast him in the role of rescuer instead of companion. In doing so, I handed him a job application for a position no man is qualified to fill.

What I didn't realize at the time was that a part of me was still operating in the **WIIFM** victim mindset: *"What's in it for me?"*

If someone came to rescue me, I wouldn't have to take responsibility for my internal chaos. I was unconsciously hoping he'd fix what only my Heavenly Creator could heal.

Let's be real. Emotional dumping on a first date is a repellent.

It sends signals of instability. It invites a man into your storm before he's had a chance to experience your peace.

I wasn't ready for a relationship then, not because I wasn't a good woman, but because I hadn't yet learned how to manage my own emotional healing. I hadn't crowned myself Queen of Peace.

Here's what I came to understand:

The men we meet on the journey to *"The One,"* can be our greatest teachers, if we're humble enough to learn. God brought several of them across my path.

The Drama Addiction

Awareness is the first step to freedom; we can't change what we don't see.

As I began noticing areas in my life that needed real change, I started recognizing a pattern, not just in myself, but in other women around me.

Women who were unknowingly operating as Chaos Queens, repeating the same emotional patterns I had, and wondering why good men kept slipping away.

Let's talk about one of them. We'll call her Diane.

Diane was a radiant force charismatic, articulate, and captivating. She was a speaker who could light up any stage and leave a room hanging on her every word. She had charm. Confidence. Power.

And she had been single for over two decades.

It wasn't because she lacked opportunities. Mr. Potentials came and went. She had no trouble attracting great men.

The problem? They'd disappear. Again, and again. Without warning. Leaving her confused and heartbroken.

> **SOMETIMES YOUR CHAOS ISN'T THE PROBLEM, IT'S THAT YOU'VE MADE IT YOUR IDENTITY.**
> ANONYMOUS

As I got to know her better, I realized something important: she was addicted to drama. She thrived on the attention and sympathy it stirred up in others.

There was always a swirling tornado of stress around her, and it pulled everyone nearby into her chaotic world.

She was **the Queen of Chaos**.

When she walked into a room, you could feel the chaotic energy trailing in behind her.

On her dates, Mr. Potential would find himself sitting through emotional monologues, someone had just died, the weather had been horrible, a loved one was sick in the hospital, and the ex was trying to sabotage her relationship with the kids, with help from his *"wicked"* new girlfriend.

Then came the friend who slept with her other friend's husband, and so on. It was the never-ending drama train, and one by one, the good guys jumped off at the next stop.

Despite her success, she couldn't see the pattern. And no, she wasn't open to feedback.

There are many reasons a woman may unknowingly operate in constant chaos. That's why it's so important to examine the emotional roots, the attention payoff, or the underlying belief systems that create this lifestyle of drama.

Now hear me clearly: it's completely normal to need comfort, counsel, or a safe place to process your pain. We all do.

But that sacred space is best reserved for your close girlfriends, a pastor, a coach, or a trusted counselor, not Mr. Potential.

A healthy man won't be drawn to a woman stuck in a state of constant drama. It's not endearing. It's exhausting.

Poor Negative Nellie

Let's look at another example, someone I'll call Negative Nellie.

At this stage in her life, Nellie was a widow who had raised four children. She was attractive, strong, good-hearted, and very devoted to helping others. She longed to be married again and was becoming more discouraged about being single.

She kept meeting wonderful Mr. Potentials. There'd be a promising spark, and then he'd disappear.

Why?

She didn't realize that almost every conversation was laced with complaints. If it wasn't the car breaking down, it was the burst pipe that flooded her floor. The dog was sick, the mailman was rude, the coffee was cold, or the food was wrong at the restaurant.

If there were three clouds in the sky, Nellie wouldn't see the beauty, she'd see it as overcast and gloomy.

She often spoke about how she didn't have enough money because she kept giving it away to people in need. Her stress was affecting her health, and she spoke about that regularly too. Though her heart was good, she'd unknowingly become a magnet for drama, and a repellent to good men.

Underneath it all, Nellie was struggling with a lack of identity and a deep-seated need for validation. Her friends saw her as the saint who was always sacrificing. *"Oh, poor Nellie,"* they'd say, *"she's always helping everyone, but life keeps throwing her curveballs."*

But what no one wanted to admit was this: Nellie was getting emotional attention through her chaos.

Do you see the pattern?

These women, whether successful or sweet, outgoing or nurturing, were unknowingly repelling healthy, emotionally available men.

But here's the hopeful truth: patterns can be changed.

And it all starts with one thing, awareness.

Chaos Check-In: Are You Attracting Drama or Healing?

Let's take a moment for some real self-reflection.

This is not to bring guilt or shame, but to bring you closer to clarity and breakthrough. Think of it as a heart tune-up.

Use the checklist below to increase your conversation awareness. Are there any patterns of **the Queen of Chaos** behaviors that you might be unconsciously operating in?

If you find yourself nodding *"yes"* to any of these, celebrate that awareness! That means you're ready to shift your romantic results and start showing up as the queen you were always meant to be.

Conversation Awareness Checklist

Check the boxes that apply to you, even occasionally:

- ☐ I find myself talking about negative situations, like who died, who's sick, who got divorced, or how awful the world is right now.
- ☐ I tend to share details about my health or finances in ways that draw attention or concern.
- ☐ I often vent about family, friends, or coworkers who've hurt or disappointed me.
- ☐ I frequently tell sad or dramatic stories when talking with others.
- ☐ I notice a pattern of wishing someone would "rescue" or fix my problems.
- ☐ I secretly enjoy the sympathy and attention I get when I share struggles.
- ☐ Complaining feels like a release, and it feels like it helps me connect with others.

- ☐ I get anxious in conversations that don't involve some kind of emotional drama.
- ☐ Calm or peaceful situations sometimes make me feel bored or disconnected.
- ☐ I bond more through negativity than through joy, purpose, or encouragement.

If you checked any boxes… that's okay. You're not alone, and you're not stuck.

Emotional chaos may have been your past, but it doesn't have to define your future. Awareness is your first breakthrough. You don't need to carry chaos to feel loved.

Homework Challenge

You're going to love this one, and it works!

For three days in a row:

1. Refrain from sharing any negative story, complaint, or drama with anyone.

Write down each negative thought or statement you catch yourself wanting to say. This will help you become aware of where your mind naturally gravitates.

_____

_____

_____

_____

_____

_____

_____

_____

_____

_____

_____

_____

_____

_____

_____

_____

2. Choose to speak life.

When you talk with people, challenge yourself to:

- Say one thing you're grateful for.
- Offer a compliment.
- Share an uplifting story

It doesn't have to be huge. Maybe you found your favorite nail polish on sale. Maybe you got the perfect parking spot. Or the sky looked especially beautiful today.

And if you don't have a personal positive story to share yet, look one up! Find a miracle story online or a testimony that lifts your spirit. Write it down below.

_____

_____

_____

_____

_____

_____

_____

_____

_____

_____

_____

3. Journal your experience below.

How did it feel to shift the energy of your conversations? What did you notice about how others responded to you? Were you more uplifted, more centered, or more connected?

And if you're feeling brave, come share your experience with us in the Solo to Soulmate Sisterhood FB group. We'd love to cheer you on!

Next, take a moment to honestly evaluate your past dates using the questions we just explored.

Did you share too much too soon?

What did your conversations revolve around? Were they balanced or mostly focused on your life?

Did you dominate the conversation without realizing it?

Were you emotionally unloading chaos, like I once did?

_____

_____

_____

_____

_____

_____

_____

_____

We're continuing to retrain your brain to speak life, embrace gratitude, and break free from the habit of negative talk.

Speak your positive declarations with ENERGY in the morning, noon, and night.

Put one hand on your heart (skin to skin) and place your other hand open in a receiving posture. With fiery passion from deep within your spirit, declare the following:

Positive Declarations

- I release myself from all drama and chaos. I welcome peace and joy into my life!
- Things come easily for me!
- Solutions present themselves to me with clarity and grace!
- I attract and receive blessings abundantly and often!

If other positive affirmations rise up in your heart, write them below. Add them to your daily routine. The more you practice these declarations, the more your mindset, and your relationships will shift. You'll not only draw in peace and favor, but also begin to attract Mr. Right.

You made it through, Queen!

And I don't just mean this chapter, I mean every emotional storm, every pattern you've bravely faced, and every moment of honest self-reflection. It takes courage to see the truth without guilt or shame. That's not weakness; that's royalty rising.

I am so proud of you.

Get ready for another eye-opener!

Have you ever found yourself trying to help a man *"reach his potential?"*

Guiding him through emotional growth?

Gently (or not-so-gently) suggesting who he could be if he just took your advice?

Do you catch yourself *"coaching"* your dates, even with good intentions?

In the next chapter, we're going to explore the subtle art of control, how it often hides behind encouragement and helpfulness and how without realizing it, this habit can quietly push good men away.

We'll talk about the man projects and discover how to lead in love... without taking over the stage.

Heart Reflections

You're doing it, beautiful one.

Another chapter conquered. More awareness gained. Growth is happening, and I'm so proud of you.

The first step to freedom is recognizing when we're caught in the cycle of chaos — and having the courage to pause and ask, *"Why?"* What's fueling the emotional whirlwind? A desire to feel seen? Validated? Connected?

When we pause long enough to ask the deeper questions, we take our power back. We stop reacting… and start responding with intention and grace.

In this chapter, you also looked honestly at how negativity — complaining, oversharing, gossiping, or emotional dumping — can become a default setting that drains our energy and quietly repels the connection our heart longs for.

But now, get ready… because your next breakthrough is waiting.

Next, we'll explore the well-meaning (but often relationship-sabotaging) habits your inner Director — Aka, the Fixer, the Backseat Driver, the woman with a plan and a color-coded spreadsheet.

Women are natural multitaskers. We can do a dozen things at once without breaking a sweat. But in romance? That same take-charge energy can unintentionally chase Mr. Right away.

Your transformation is unfolding beautifully.

Let's dive in!

Chapter Nine

THE DIRECTOR
(AKA The Backseat Driver)

> *GOD MADE ADAM FIRST BECAUSE HE DIDN'T WANT*
> *ANY UNSOLICITED ADVICE FROM EVE!*
> UNKNOWN AUTHOR

What a funny and poignant quote! But how often do we, as women, offer unsolicited advice, guidance, or feedback no one actually asked for?

We have amazing intuition. We often know what's best. And when our input is ignored, especially by a man we care about, it can feel frustrating or even dismissive.

We're also naturally wired to improve things. So, we speak up. We point out what could be better, or how something should be done differently.

Here's the catch: when those helpful instincts turn into a pattern, we risk stepping into the role of The Director, and that's where we can unknowingly repel a good man.

Who Is the Director?

The Director (a.k.a. the Backseat Driver) likes to be in control. She knows best. She's quick to correct and eager to guide. She offers commentary and critique, sometimes even before anyone asks for it. Her strength in managing people and organizing situations often masks her avoidance of deeper personal work.

At the root? Often a subconscious fear, fear of vulnerability, fear of losing control, fear of being hurt.

And without realizing it, she deactivates a man's superhero wiring by making him feel incompetent, unworthy, or unappreciated.

Remember... good men want to be your superhero. They want to feel trusted, needed, and appreciated, not micromanaged.

It's easy to forget that men are wired differently than women. Sometimes, we fall into the **WIIFM** mindset: *What's In It For Me?* We assume our needs matter more. But healthy love isn't about control. It's about mutual respect.

Often, the urge to direct or *"fix"* others reveals a deeper desire to validate ourselves. It can also be a way to avoid healing from past wounds or facing uncomfortable truths in our own hearts.

And let's not forget that what we say shapes the direction of our lives.

The Man-Project

A different variation of the Director is the woman who takes on Man-Projects. She chooses men based on their potential and gets to work on *"improving"* them. Her identity becomes wrapped up in what she's building, not in who she is.

There's a false sense of purpose in *"bettering"* Mr. Potential. It feels like love, but it's really a subtle form of control.

We often do this when:

- We're afraid of getting hurt.
- We want to feel needed.
- We fear rejection from someone who's already *"whole."*
- We don't fully believe we're worthy of a truly healthy man.

By choosing someone who needs us, we feel safe. But it's an illusion. **Because here's the truth: trying to fix a man is not love, it's self-protection dressed in sacrificial disguise.**

And it's deeply unfair to him.

Trying to change a man or *"make him better"* for our own emotional security is not partnership, it's a power play. And ultimately, it hurts both people. Been there done that.

Are You Controlling or Helping?

Let's break it down with a few real-life examples of man-project behaviors:

- You drive long distances to see him, but he won't do the same for you.
- You help him find a therapist, rebuild his credit, and hand him money while he's finishing school.
- You cook, clean, organize, hoping your efforts will mold him into the man you need.
- You remind him how much you've done for him, subtly (or not so subtly) implying he *"owes"* you.
- You feel responsible for his success or personal growth. In your mind, you made him better.

But in his heart? He may feel belittled, controlled, or emasculated. And when a man feels that way long enough, he starts seeking validation somewhere else, from someone who simply sees and accepts him.

We've all heard the story:

"I just want someone who appreciates me."

Boss Betty

Let's look at a woman we'll call Betty.

147

She was in her sixties, married for 35 years. One day, *out of the blue*, her husband told her he wanted a divorce and admitted there was another woman.

Quick side note: Is adultery ok? Absolutely not. What we are doing here is unpacking how things led up to that point. We are looking at the woman's side of the coin.

Naturally Betty was crushed. *"How could he do this to me after **everything** I've done for him!?"* she asked. And it's true, she had sacrificed a lot. She supported him through medical school, helped build his practice, and managed the office with an iron fist.

All her friends said she was a saint of a wife.

Remember…there are two sides to every marriage, and both spouses contribute to the failure of the marriage. So, let's unpack her story a little deeper and we'll see another truth emerge:

What Betty didn't tell her friends is that for years, Betty had unintentionally made her husband feel inferior.

She regularly reminded him of how ***she made him*** the man he was. That her sacrifices were responsible for ***all*** his success. That **she** (not we) built the life they had. And while it wasn't all untrue, it wasn't all of the truth either.

Yes, she worked hard, but so did he. He graduated med school, he worked very hard to build the practice, take care of his family and patients.

She consistently reminded him of what he was doing wrong or what he should do better. In public and private she would belittle him.

Do you recognize these superhero deactivators?

Naturally he didn't feel seen for his contributions, felt consistently disrespected and criticized. Multiply this by 30 + years.

Over time, her words and actions chipped away at his self-worth. He felt like he could never measure up and nothing he did was good enough. So when someone else came along who affirmed him and made him feel appreciated, the pull was too strong to ignore.

Betty wasn't emotionally mature enough to evaluate why she always needed to be right, why she always needed validation.

But like many of us, she lacked awareness in the moment, and by the time she understood, it was too late.

My Own Director Days

As women, we may try to change someone because we need to make changes within ourselves but aren't aware of it. It makes us feel good about ourselves because we're "helping better" someone else.

Another reason we may gravitate toward man-projects is from a deeper, hidden fear of getting hurt. Or a deeper lack of unworthiness.

I played The Director role in various ways too.

Looking back, I often chose *"man-projects,"* not out of love, but out of fear. Fear of rejection. Fear of unworthiness. Fear of giving my heart to a great man and he wouldn't want me.

Man-projects felt safe. If I had to fix him, then I held the power.

If I could control his journey, I wouldn't be vulnerable.

But that's not love. That's a form of selfishness and fear.

At the time, I didn't know my true worth.

I thought, if I can just improve him, he'll become the perfect man for me. Seeing a pattern?

My identity was wrapped up in being the Savior. And it felt good, until it didn't.

Derek: The Muffin Top Makeover

Years after my divorce, I met a genuinely nice guy named Derek.

But in my eyes? He needed a little *"fixin'."* He became my Man-Project.

As we were getting to know each other, I would direct him with suggestions on how he could improve himself. I offered unsolicited advice by recommending self-help books and researching good therapists he could choose from.

Oh yes, I was the all-knowing one. When he made mistakes, I was quick to point out what he did wrong and let him know what a bad mistake it was.

I also utilized my administrative skills and created menus designed to help him lose the muffin top. I bought him different styles of clothes I knew would look better. What was in his closet was frumpy. In my supreme wisdom, I even offered suggestions on fat-burning workout routines. In addition, there was a great special at the gym he should join.

Does this sound familiar? Do you find yourself choosing man-projects, men you try to fix or improve?

Do you regularly offer *"expert"* opinions or unsolicited advice on what he or others in his life should do differently?

That was me. And it didn't go over well.

To my surprise, Derek, yes, my muffin-top-fixing, "man-project," finally exploded one day. After enduring my constant critiques and "helpful advice," he snapped. Loud, irritated, and visibly frustrated, he said:

*"Why are we always talking about what **I need to fix** about myself? Why don't we talk about what **you** need to change? Why can't you just accept me for who I am?"*

Then came the real sting:

"What if I told you that you need to lose weight, fix the wrinkles on your face, and buy nicer clothes? How would you feel if I told you to stop stuffing your face with cookies and ice cream, get rid of your muffin top, and go work out? Why are you even dating me?"

OUCH!

The air went still. I sat in stunned silence, not knowing what to say.

But here's the truth, he was right.

I hadn't accepted him for who he was. I hadn't affirmed the good in him. I was so focused on what needed *"fixin'"* that I made him feel unattractive, criticized, and unworthy. Was that my intention? Absolutely not.

In my mental matrix, I believed I was helping him become his best self. In reality, I was playing the role of the backseat driver, the man-breaker.

And here's the thing: how we do anything often bleeds into other areas of our lives.

If I could do this in a romantic relationship, how many others had I unintentionally hurt or diminished with my *"help"*?

I'll say this, Derek showed tremendous emotional courage that day.

He drew a boundary and called out behavior that most men would've internalized in silence or walked away from altogether.

And I'm so grateful he did.

Had I not been in a teachable place, I might've lashed out. I could've defensively thrown my sacrifices in his face, screaming, *"After everything I've done for you!"* But by then, I had learned how to be coachable.

So I listened. I apologized. I took full responsibility. And I affirmed the good in him.

He forgave me, and though we chose not to pursue a romantic relationship, we remained friends.

In fact, we're still good friends today.

Gentle reminder: The men we meet along the path to Mr. Right can be some of our best teachers, if we let them.

The Sugar Mamma

Let's look at a more extreme example of The Director at work.

We'll call her Louise. She invited her boyfriend, William, to move in with her while he pursued law school. Though he offered to contribute financially, rent, groceries, utilities, she refused. She wanted to take care of it all herself so he could focus on his studies.

Now, that sounds sweet and sacrificial, right?

But here's the hidden problem: her *"generosity"* gave her complete financial control. And control was the real currency of the relationship.

She directed everything, what needed to be done, when, and how. She even criticized him when he used his own money to buy groceries, especially if he bought the *"wrong"* things. Her martyrdom became her **WIIFM** (*What's In It For Me*), a source of pride, praise, and validation from her friends who admired her selflessness.

But at home? Louise constantly reminded William how much she was doing for him. She made him feel small, incapable, and dependent.

This relationship dynamic slowly crushed his confidence.

And eventually, halfway through law school, William left, like a flash of lightning.

He couldn't take it anymore.

Louise, of course, was devastated.

She told everyone:

"After everything I did for him! I can't believe he used me and left me like that!"

She blamed him.

She painted herself as the victim.

But she never took responsibility for her controlling, demeaning, and emasculating behavior.

She was a man-breaker and never realized it.

The Truth About Control

Did Louise make William feel like a superhero?

No. She clipped his wings.

She rejected his offers to contribute. She dismissed his efforts. She rejected his masculinity, his desire to provide, lead, and stand as an equal partner.

What could she have done differently?

For starters, not inviting him to move in might have preserved a healthy balance of independence and leadership. But even after that choice, she still had the opportunity to affirm and partner with him instead of controlling him.

William wasn't lazy. He was a hard-working man pursuing a grueling degree.

Instead of micromanaging his every move, Louise could have shown gratitude for his efforts:

"Thanks for picking up groceries."

"I see how hard you're working. I'm proud of you."

"Let's budget together so we both feel supported."

He didn't need a manager. He needed a woman who believed in him.

A woman who let him lead in his own way. A woman who respected his strength and gave him space to grow.

But Louise couldn't do that. Her **WIIFM** mindset, the need for attention, control, and to be *"needed"* ran the show.

And it cost her a potentially great relationship.

From Director to Queen

Ladies, we are the queens on the chessboard.

We hold power and influence.

We can be kingmakers, or man-breakers.

If you see yourself in any form of The Director, whether through micromanagement, martyrdom, or fixing "man-projects," it's time to stop and re-evaluate. Ask yourself: *Why do I feel the need to control?*

What is my emotional payoff for always *"helping"* or directing? Is it rooted in fear, insecurity, pride, or ego?

These are tough questions, but they lead to true freedom.

Awareness is the first step.

Taking responsibility is the next. Transformation follows.

You don't need to shame yourself. You just need to get honest with yourself.

Congratulations, beautiful, you've made it this far in the book, and I'm so proud of you!

You are showing tremendous courage and humility by being willing to grow.

In the next chapter, let's dive into how that *"harmless competition"* between men and women can quietly shift, turning playful banter into power struggles. And when ego leads, even the strongest crowns can lose their balance.

But first, let's dive into this chapter's thought reflections and homework assignment.

I'd love for you to share your insights and *"aha!"* moments on the FB Solo to Soulmate Sisterhood page. We want to cheer you on!

Thought Reflections

Let's take a quick, honest inventory of the inner you.

On a scale of 1 (low) to 10 (high), how strong is your tendency to direct or backseat drive in relationships?

1 2 3 4 5 6 7 8 9 10 *(Circle One)*

Do you offer unsolicited advice or feedback on what a man (or others) need to change?

List two recent examples where you did this:

_____

_____

_____

_____

_____

_____

Do you gravitate toward Man-Projects?
Let's take a moment to get honest with ourselves.
What kinds of things are you doing for your current (or past) Man-Project?

- Are you: Supporting him financially?
- Acting as his emotional coach?
- Paying for his gas, groceries, bills, or even his therapy or coaching sessions?
- Taking control of the household or finances?

Now dig a little deeper.

What's the emotional payoff you're getting from doing all this?

_____

_____

_____

_____

_____

_____

What mistakes have you made in trying to control, direct, or

"fix" someone else? Journal below.

Then, as you feel led, take the courageous step to apologize where it's appropriate and safe to do so. Even a simple, sincere, _"I realize I overstepped, and I'm sorry,"_ can be deeply healing, for you and for them.

_____

_____

_____

_____

_____

_____

_____

_____

_____

Homework Assignment

For the next three days, I want to challenge you to do something powerful.

Apply what I lovingly call *"spiritual duct tape"* to your mouth.

Begin to intentionally observe yourself and make a conscious effort to pause before offering unsolicited advice, correction, or instruction to anyone, whether it's a friend, coworker, child, or even a stranger at the grocery store.

Instead of jumping in with suggestions or solutions, simply listen. Breathe. Hold space.

This is your awareness challenge.

Each time you catch yourself about to *"fix,"* direct, or offer guidance no one asked for, jot it down in your journal.

- What was the situation?
- What did you want to say?
- How did it feel to hold back?

You may be surprised by how often we operate in *"helping"* mode out of habit, not realizing it might be more about our own need for control than the other person's need for direction.

At the end of the three days, reflect on what you learned. Did you feel more peaceful? More present? Did anyone respond differently when you simply listened instead of instructed?

This isn't about being passive. It's about creating space for others to rise, and for yourself to grow in wisdom, restraint, and grace.

I always give myself permission to change my mind when I receive new insight. That mindset has been life-changing for me, because it opened the door to seeing things from a fresh perspective.

Being coachable will take you far in life. Give yourself permission to change your mind.

The path of truth is lighting up before you, and you're walking it beautifully! You're moving through these exercises like a champ, and I couldn't be prouder of your willingness and courage to acknowledge areas in your life that may need a little adjusting.

Here's something powerful to consider: the word *repent* simply means *to change your mind.*

Isn't that encouraging?

Growth isn't about shame, it's about shifting. It's about turning toward something better.

You're doing an amazing job.

Now, let's dive into how that *"harmless competition"* between men and women can quietly shift, turning playful banter into subtle power struggles. And when ego leads instead of grace, even the strongest crowns can lose their balance.

Heart Reflections
FROM JOANNA

Congratulations, beautiful one — you're doing it.

With each chapter, you're shedding old habits and stepping more fully into the graceful, powerful woman God created you to be.

Constant correcting, advising, or directing doesn't empower them... it unintentionally sends the message that they're incapable. That's not love. That's management.

You also uncovered the deeper roots behind the urge to fix, rescue, or "shape" a man — whether it comes from wanting control or feeling safer when we lead.

Now you're recognizing those tendencies, releasing the fixer role, and stepping into your true identity as a **Kingmaker**, not a director.

And that brings us to the next relationship-sabotaging behavior — one of the sneakiest ways strong women repel healthy love without even realizing it.

In the next chapter, we'll meet **The One-Upper** *(The Competitor)* — the brilliant woman who brings her boardroom energy into the ballroom of romance... and ends up dancing alone.

It's time to explore how competition can quietly crush connection — and how letting go of the need to be right opens the door to being truly loved.

Are you ready? Let's turn the page.

Chapter Ten

THE ONE-UPPER
(AKA The Competitor)

And then men end the conversation with, *"Yes, dear!"* All jokes aside, let's take a closer look at the subtle, and not-so-subtle forms of one-upping that stem from this dynamic and how they can unintentionally repel a good man.

Before we dive in, take a moment to reflect.

Do you find yourself one-upping a man in areas like money, wit, intelligence, or status?

Would you say you're usually right, or at least feel the need to be?

As a successful career woman, athlete, or high achiever, do you find yourself unconsciously competing with Mr. Potential?

Do you carry an underlying need to prove yourself in relationships?

Certain roles in life require us to show up strong, assertive, and driven.

- As a competitive athlete, you're trained to win.

- As a military commander, you must be decisive and tough.
- As a business owner or executive, you juggle deadlines, team management, and fierce competition.
- As a mother, you're the problem-solver, schedule-keeper, and voice of reason in the household.

But if we're not mindful, that same edge can follow us into our romantic lives, and it doesn't always translate well.

Let's look at what happens when the *"One-Upper"* (a.k.a. The Competitor) shows up out of balance:

- She often needs the last word.
- She's quick to correct or dismiss opinions that differ from hers.
- She may unconsciously argue a point until her man gives up and mutters, *"Yes, dear."*
- She struggles to apologize or to accept her man for who he is, flaws, gifts, and all.
- She compares her wins and achievements with his, rather than celebrating both.
- She resists receiving help, like letting him carry the groceries or open her door, because she believes she can do it better.

Sound familiar?

These behaviors aren't always born from pride.

Often, they're rooted in something deeper: feelings of unworthiness, the need to prove we belong, or a belief that being vulnerable isn't safe.

- Maybe she had to be *"the strong one"* just to survive.

- Maybe she grew up in a home where love was earned, not freely given, where criticism was common and approval was rare.
- Maybe she learned to hold her own among brothers or had to succeed in a male-dominated world where emotions were seen as weakness.

Over time, competition became her armor, her way of never feeling small again.

But here's the real question, Queen:

Are you still wearing that armor in your relationships?

Is your need to be right, to correct, or to prove yourself, keeping love at arm's length?

Let me be real with you. I know this struggle personally.

As a little girl, I was a full-blown tomboy. I raced the boys on bikes, competed fiercely, and had to prove I was just as tough, if not tougher than them. I'd argue, wrestle, even name and shame. It gave me an identity, and a false sense of safety.

"Anything you can do, I can do better" wasn't just a song, it was my life motto.

That mindset quietly followed me into womanhood.

I made my own money. I bought my own cars. Handled my own business. I was proud of my independence, and rightfully so.

But in dating?

That same mindset began to sabotage my connections with men.

I didn't mean to, but I ended up competing with Mr. Potential instead of connecting with him. I didn't make him feel seen, respected, or valued. Instead of honoring him, I argued with him.

If he had an opinion I disagreed with, I'd debate it until he gave up.

It was a variation of **WIIFM** *(What's In It For Me?)*, because it became all about my thoughts, my feelings, and my need to be right.

His ideas didn't matter, and I unknowingly made him feel dismissed and inferior.

That's not what I intended, but it's what I was doing. It was ego. It was armor.

And it's not the way to a soulmate.

> ### *THE LAST WORD MIGHT WIN THE MOMENT, BUT HUMILITY WINS THE HEART.*
> ANONYMOUS

There's a big difference between playful, lighthearted competition between partners, and the kind of competitive energy that slowly deactivates a man's inner Superman.

When the drive to one-up becomes chronic, it changes the atmosphere. The relationship shifts from intimacy to insecurity. And over time, it can quietly erode trust, connection, and respect.

Our words create our worlds, and they influence the world of the man we're in relationship with.

Here's a sobering truth to consider: millions of men struggle with loneliness every single week.

Let that sink in — every week. And that loneliness rooted in rejection?

It doesn't just sit quietly in the corner, it often drives men into hidden places. One of the most common? Pornography.

Let me be clear: This is not an excuse for porn use or other unhealthy behavior. Not at all.

But it is a lens, a way of understanding what's often going on beneath the surface. Many men don't turn to porn just out of lust. They turn to it out of emotional avoidance.

It becomes a way to escape deeper feelings of depression, rejection, isolation, or low self-worth. For many, it's not about desire, it's about pain.

At the root of every addiction is a longing for love, and often, an inability or unwillingness to face the ache beneath it.

So why are we talking about this in a chapter on competition?

Because our words matter. Because when we constantly challenge, correct, or compete with a man, especially one we love, we may be echoing the same judgment or rejection he's already carrying silently inside.

We tend to think men are made of steel. That their armor deflects our words like arrows. That they don't really hear us, or if they do, they brush it off.

But that's not true.

They may not always show it, but they feel it. Deeply.

So here's the question:

Are your words building him up, or breaking him down?

I share this not to shame, but to empower. Because understanding this changes everything.

Let's flip the script for a second.

How do you feel when someone constantly argues with you or corrects you? Or they point out your mistakes. Worse, they rarely apologize and make you feel foolish for disagreeing with them.

Not great, right?

So how often do we, without realizing it, do this to the men in our lives?

The Ugly Dating Truth... A Different Perspective

As I shared earlier, I interviewed several men while writing this book. I wanted to hear their honest experiences, to gain insight from their side of the story. And what they revealed was powerful, raw, and eye-opening.

One man shared something that stopped me in my tracks.

"When a woman constantly makes a man feel small, inferior, or like he can never measure up," he said, *"sometimes he just wants to feel like he can do something right."* So he sleeps with her, which becomes his win. Then he disappears. That's called the 'hump and dump'.

Read that again.

For him, getting her into bed wasn't just about sex, it was about validation.

It's a final, twisted victory. A way to reclaim a shred of confidence or control.

She may have thought she held the power in that moment, but she didn't. The truth is she got used. She was wrung out like a rag and tossed aside.

She's still single. Still wondering, *"What just happened? Or I sure got him."*

Is it right? No. Is it fair? Absolutely not. But it is real.

Nobody wins in these scenarios. She demeans him. He uses her. And then he walks away, only to commit to the next woman who does respect him.

It's a dysfunctional cycle, but sadly, one that plays out far too often.

If this has ever happened to you, let me say this with love and truth:

Don't shame yourself. Don't beat yourself up.

This is a wake-up call, not your worth. If you feel like you need some prayer, go to *Appendix A.*

You are not disposable. You are not someone's ego boost or escape.

You are a daughter of the King.

Your body, your time, your heart, they are sacred.

Weaponized Competition

Let's go one layer deeper.

The Competitor doesn't always show up in obvious ways. Sometimes, she uses control, criticism, or sex as tools to manipulate or dominate.

Many women don't realize that this kind of unhealthy competition is a form of emotional abuse.

She might withhold affection, affirmations, or intimacy as punishment.

She may believe she's *"teaching him a lesson"*, but what she's really doing is breaking him down. Silencing his voice. Making him feel unworthy.

These are man-breaking behaviors. Superhero deactivators.

This isn't about assigning blame. This is about empowering healing.

If you're reading this and feeling a little triggered... it's okay.

Breathe. Go take a walk and pray.

Come back when you're ready.

You're doing brave, beautiful work! Keep going!

You're looking in the mirror, asking the hard questions, and choosing a new path forward. That's growth. That's courage. That's how freedom begins.

In my first marriage, I had trauma to heal from. And while it would've been easy to point fingers and say, *"It was all his fault."*

I knew that blame wouldn't free me, it would keep me stuck in the same cycle. Wash. Rinse. Repeat. Same man. Different name. Same pain.

Yes, I could've stayed bitter. I could've made excuses. I could've kept choosing wounded men and called it bad luck.

But instead, I turned inward.

I took responsibility for my motives. My mindset. My choices.

And that's where everything changed. That's where freedom began.

And reading this book?

That's where your freedom begins too.

Ms. Nothing is Good Enough

My friend, we'll call him *"Joe,"* once dated a woman who embodied The Competitor. Let's call her Nancy. She was a pro at one-upping and pointing out what he could have done better.

If Joe bought her a beautiful bouquet, she'd comment that the colors weren't her favorite.

If he gave her a heartfelt card, she'd complain that he didn't write enough. She never acknowledged that he took time out of his day to go to the store, choose a card, and write something meaningful.

No matter what he did, she always had a subtle dig or complaint. It was never good enough.

When he took her to a five-star restaurant, she'd nitpick the menu or critique the food.

She even blamed him for the bad things that happened in her life.

Did the relationship work out?

Uh, no.

Then there was my other friend, we'll call him *"John",* who went on a date with a woman he thought might be his dream girl. Let's just say she turned out to be Ms. Wrong.

John owned a high-end jewelry store and had a great eye for fine pieces. He took her to a romantic, elegant restaurant. As they talked, he glanced at her necklace, admiring its craftsmanship.

Before he could say a word, she suddenly began waving her hands wildly and pointed furiously from her chest to her face. In a loud, obnoxious tone she yelled,

"Hey! Up here! You can talk to my face, not these!"

The entire restaurant went silent. People turned to stare.

John was mortified.

The truth?

He wasn't looking at her body. He was admiring her necklace.

Speechless, he just sat there while she gave him a smug look of superiority, clearly proud of having *"put him in his place."* In public.

He never went out with her again.

But the damage was done.

John walked away not just hurt, but mistrustful of women. Afraid of being misjudged, humiliated, or demeaned again.

This is exactly what I meant earlier when I talked about man-breaking behaviors. Superhero deactivators.

When women operate from insecurity, superiority, or unhealed wounds, they can unintentionally damage the very men who are trying to show up well.

So how are you treating the men on your journey?

Are you allowing room for imperfection, for grace?

Or do your expectations leave no space for mistakes? One upping during arguments.

Let's talk about a subtle, often overlooked form of competition in relationships: one-upping during conflict.

Sure, it's easy to spot one upping in casual conversations, topping stories, correcting facts, or proving how we're always a little more right than the other person.

But there's a quieter version of it that many of us (myself included) have practiced:

Doing it during disagreements.

You know what I mean: He messes up, and we say, *"Well, you should have"* Or *"See? I told you."*

It's a subtle power play. We're not resolving the issue; we're winning the conflict.

But "the win" costs us something far more valuable: intimacy, trust, and connection.

This is where your emotional intelligence gets tested.

Remember back in Chapter Three? We explored emotional intelligence as a hidden love superpower. Here's where it really shines, in how we handle conflict.

When a man makes a mistake, our goal isn't to shame him.

It's to build a bridge of understanding.

That begins with what I call the *Anti-Defensive Technique*:

Remove the word *"you"* from the opening line.

Why?

Because when you start with *"You did"* or *"You should have,"* his defenses go up.

Walls rise. Connection drops.

Instead, assume the best. He's not your enemy, and you're not his. Speak from the belief that he didn't intend to disappoint or hurt you.

And if you're truly upset, give yourself time to process.

Pray. Journal. Take a walk.

Then circle back to the conversation, calmly and privately.

(Yes, privately… Never correct or confront a man in public. That's a fast track to shrinking his masculinity.)

A Better Way to Speak Up

Let's look at a simple shift:

Instead of: *"You forgot to call me!"*

Try: *"Hey, I was really looking forward to hearing from you today. Everything okay?"*

That soft reframe communicates concern, not condemnation.

When something frustrates you, don't lead with criticism. Lead with compassion or curiosity, not correction and accusation.

Some examples of asking inquisitively, not accusatorily, are:

- *Help me understand what happened there.*
- *I know your heart; this just caught me off guard. Can we talk about it?*

These simple shifts speak life, not lessons, and they change everything.

It opens the door to honest dialogue instead of shutting him down.

If love is the goal, connection matters more than being right.

A Real-Life Example: Me and David

When my husband David and I were dating, I had a chance to practice this.

One day, during a phone call, he asked me to hold while he took another call. But he never came back. I stayed on hold for several minutes, then finally hung up.

It happened again the next day. I was irritated, of course, but I also knew I needed to handle it with maturity and love.

So, I waited until we were in a calm space. After some small talk, I gently brought it up.

Joanna: *"I know you're super busy, and I totally understand if you need to step away from a call. Could you do me a favor?"*

David: *"Sure. What is it?"*

Joanna: *"Next time we're talking and you need to hop off, would you just let me know? The past two times, I was left on the eternal hold and wasn't sure if you'd be back. I waited about five minutes before hanging up and felt a little disrespected. I know that's not your heart, I know you'd never intentionally do that."*

David (pause): *"You're right. I'm sorry. I had an urgent prayer call, and I just assumed you knew. But I see how that could have come across. I'll let you know next time."*

Do you see the power of how I spoke to him? And how he responded?

If I had snapped, *"You're so rude! You left me hanging again!"*

He would have been put on the defensive and seen it as a red flag. If I had assumed he "did it on purpose' and accuse him, as a healthy man, it would have been offensive because that wasn't his heart or intention.

Sometimes it's not what you say, it's how you say it. Women can get that snarky, accusatory tone.

Little keys unlock big doors. And big doors swing on small hinges.

The Ballroom Pole Test!

Let me give you a fun example, and yes, it involves a pole!

(Stay with me)

There was a season when I took up ballroom dancing. I became a graceful, seasoned dancer over time. But of course, not everyone in class was at the same level.

One day, I was paired with a sweet guy named Greg, who was clearly new and very nervous. During a spin, he missed my hand and sent me reeling, straight into a pole.

OUCH!

Then, on our next pass across the dance floor, he backed me into the same pole again. Can you say *"OUCH"!*

The old me would have snapped: "Are you blind? How could you not see that pole?! What's wrong with you?!"

But instead, I paused, I took a breath. And I smiled.

"That pole has it out for me today! I joked. *"But hey, you nailed those other moves."*

I'll never forget the look on Greg's face. He went from expecting to be berated and yelled at to shocked and relieved at the same time.

His eyes lit up and was so happy.

And you know what happened? He got better. He kept dancing. He left that day encouraged.

If I had embarrassed or berated him, he might've never come back.

Worse, he might've carried that shame into future relationships.

Remember, it takes a lot of courage for a guy to try something he's not good at and risk rejection, failure and humiliation.

Ladies, the Queen protects the King.

If you recognize yourself in any part of The Competitor, now's the time to gently self-reflect.

This isn't about shame, it's about awareness.

You can't change what you won't acknowledge.

We can't become a better version of ourselves if we aren't aware, right?

If we don't know what needs to be adjusted, we can't practice the courage to change. In the next chapter, we are going to cover the last of the relationship personality behaviors that can cost a woman years of her life with Mr. Wrong or keep her single for a long time.

Practical Application

Fun Quiz: A Touch of the One Upper

It takes time to develop new patterns of behavior: inch by inch, it's a cinch.

Awareness and honesty are the gateways to growth. You're a champion for even showing up here!

Take a few moments to reflect on the questions below. Be honest with yourself. This is about awareness, not shame. No guilt, just growth.

Check any that apply to you:

- ☐ When someone shares good news, do you often respond with, *"That reminds me of when I"*, and shift the spotlight back to you?
- ☐ Do you feel the urge to prove your point, even if it means arguing until the last word is yours?
- ☐ In conflict, do you lead with phrases like *"You should have"* or *"You always"* to prove you were right?
- ☐ Do you secretly (or not-so-secretly) enjoy being the smartest person in the room?
- ☐ When a man shares something vulnerable or emotional, do you instantly respond with your own story or pain, trying to match or out-emotion him?
- ☐ Do you feel the need to correct others' facts, grammar, opinions, even in casual conversations?
- ☐ When a man makes a mistake, do you replay it (even subtly) to remind him you were right?
- ☐ Do you struggle to compliment others without mentally adding, *"But I've done something even better"?*
- ☐ Do you sometimes feel threatened or competitive when a man succeeds or takes the lead?
- ☐ Do you unintentionally interrupt or finish people's sentences to *"speed things along"* (especially when you already know where it's going)?

Scoring Key:

♦ **0–2: The Graceful Supporter**

Confident, calm, and no need to compete. Keep shining, Queen!

♦ **3–5: The Recovering Rival**

Old habits may whisper, but wisdom is rising. Stay the course, you're doing the work.

♦ 6–8: **The Friendly Firecracker**

There's power in your passion, just direct it toward partnership, not performance. You've got this!

♦ 9–10: **The Queen of Comparison**

You're not alone, and you're not stuck. Healing begins when you stop proving and start embracing your worth. Let God rewrite the script.

Awareness Reflections:

    A. What moment in your past taught you that you had to earn love by being right, smart, or strong?
    B. What would it look like to release that belief and rest in the truth that you are enough, just as you are?

Self-Awareness Exercise:

This practice is all about conscious growth. For the next three days, monitor how often you:

- Feel the need to correct.
- Prove a point.
- Compete in conversation.

Use the space below to jot down your observations.

Day One: _____

Day Two: _____

Day Three: _____

Growth Tip: The next time you feel the urge to *"correct," "prove,"* or *"top"* someone's story...

Pause. Smile. Ask yourself: *"Is this a moment to connect or to compete?"*

Words Matter

How we speak to men, and everyone in our lives has the power to either build them up or break them down often without us even realizing it.

Reflect Honestly:

- Do I often default to pointing out what he missed or could've done better?
- Do I unintentionally *"coach"* my partner instead of appreciating him?
- Do I feel safer in control than I do in vulnerability?

Final Reflection:

- What fear, belief, or past experience drives your need to take the lead or *"fix"* things?
- What would happen if you let go of the need to be right or have the last word?

You're doing the deep, beautiful work of transformation. You're not just becoming the woman who finds love, you're becoming the woman who knows she's worthy of it.

_____

_____

_____

_____

_____

_____

_____

_____

_____

You should be feeling incredibly proud of yourself right now!

How does this transformation process feel for you? I found it to be very liberating.

Give us a shout out on the FB Solo to Soulmate Sisterhood page.

Layer by layer, you're becoming the enhanced, radiant version of you. That takes courage, honesty, and heart. You are part of the Courage Club!

We discussed how subtle or not so subtle competition, especially in the form of needing to be right, have the last word, or out-share, can slowly erode connection and trust with a good man.

- You recognized the difference between healthy confidence and the subtle control that can unintentionally emasculate a man.
- You learned how your words and tone, especially in conflict — can build a bridge or burn one. Queen's reminder: **speak life, not lessons**.
- And you're mastering how to confront with honor, ask inquisitively not accusatorily and lead with empathy over ego.

Are you ready to look at the mistake that can cost a woman years of her life with the wrong man or miss out on being with Mr. Right? It's something so simple, yet profound.

Keep reading, the best is yet to come!

Chapter Eleven

THE FANTASIZER
(Falling for Fantasy Not Reality)

> *EMOTIONALLY INACCESSIBLE IS HOW SOME*
> *DESCRIBE IT. I REFER TO IT AS "A CHALLENGE."*
> ANONYMOUS

How many of us have met someone who appeared to be Prince Charming, only to discover he was really Mr. Toad in disguise? How often have we gotten involved with a man, only to look back and wonder what we ever found attractive about him?

Why do we do this?

One of the most common and heartbreaking traps I see women fall into is choosing **fantasy** over **reality**.

- What causes some of us to fall for a man who is emotionally unavailable, or worse, married and clearly off-limits?
- Why do we spend our time and energy chasing him, trying to win him over?
- What deeper belief within us drives this pattern?

There's often a part of us that doesn't want to face the truth.

A part that resists looking into the deeper wells of our own soul. And unless we heal that space, this mindset will quietly block us from attracting the man God truly has for us.

Trust me, I've been there. I've also watched too many women fall for the fantasy and pay a steep emotional price.

When we choose fantasy, we can waste months, sometimes years on a path that only leads to heartbreak, self-doubt, and baggage that takes time to unpack.

Here's the harsh truth: only about 3–5% of married men actually leave their wives for another woman. The odds are slim, and the cost is high.

We can end up entangled in a toxic marriage, like I did, or miss out on the beautiful story God was writing with Mr. Right, because we were too distracted by Mr. Wrong.

So why do women fall for fantasy over reality?

There are several deeply rooted, often subconscious reasons. Let's look at a few:

- A feeling of unworthiness or fear of getting hurt again.
- To avoid vulnerability, she unconsciously chooses someone who's emotionally unavailable, someone who'll never truly touch her heart, because it feels safer.
- She's in love with the idea of marriage more than the man.
- She may believe a relationship will finally fill the void that only God can fill. (Remember the Elizabeth Taylor example from The Hidden Love Superpower chapter?)
- Desperation is rooted in a need to be rescued.

This can stem from childhood wounds, broken dreams, or abandonment.

The emotional toll of unfulfilled dreams — especially when singleness stretches longer than expected — can lead to a deep ache of loneliness and despair. And in that vulnerable place, fantasy becomes tempting.

Why do women often chase a married man or an emotionally unavailable one?

Because, on a subconscious level, she may believe that a good man of her own doesn't exist... or that she isn't worthy of one. She may fear rejection from a man who *could* love her. Or she may envy another woman who did the inner work, received the reward, and wonders why she didn't.

Let's talk about deferred hope for a moment. Have you felt it?

It's real. It shows up in the quiet corners of life, often after waiting longer than you planned for love, marriage, or family. Over time, it can leave you sad, discouraged, and afraid your dreams won't come true.

"Hope deferred makes the heart sick." — Proverbs 13:12 (KJV)

If this resonates with you, you're not alone. Every woman encounters deferred hope at some point. But awareness is the key — because from awareness, you can choose differently. (For deeper healing around this, see Appendix A.)

When we've been rejected, lonely, or repeatedly disappointed, it becomes easy to ignore the truth about a man, even when it is starring right at us.

Here's the good news! You're love story is being re-written and God is healing your soul.

Here's what I've learned over time that helped me see truth about whether I can trust someone:

People often tell us exactly who they are and often times in a "joking" way.

But we miss it, because we're too busy believing who we want them to be.

This is your moment of awakening, Queen. **The truth doesn't hurt, it heals.** And healing clears the way for healthy, God ordained love. You deserve that kind of love.

DATING HIS POTENTIAL

I wasn't dating a man, I was dating his potential

NOT LOOKING FOR ANYTHING SERIOUS

When he said, "I'm not ready for a relationship," I heard, 'I can change him."

When the deeper wells of unmet emotional needs go unaddressed, we can unknowingly choose blindness.

We overlook red flags, excuse inconsistent behavior, and attach ourselves to his potential rather than his reality.

The result? We waste our time, energy, and heart on Mr. Unavailable, chasing what could be instead of accepting what actually is.

But here's the truth: Clarity is power.

And the moment we choose truth over fantasy, we step into freedom.

As you know, when I first met my ex-Mr. Wrong, he appeared to be everything I thought I wanted. He was funny, successful, caring, had a servant's heart, liked to dance, and seemed like Prince Charming.

But the reality?

I had chosen a man who had a casual relationship with the truth, was a secret alcoholic, betrayed my trust, and caused deep emotional damage.

I wasted precious time and energy on this man, and repelled the good, solid, emotionally available men in the process.

I allowed myself to be pressured into marriage instead of waiting on God's timing. Had I listened to the red flags and honored my inner voice, my story might have had a very different beginning.

The good news? God is a Redeemer. He turns our mistakes into miracles. And if He hadn't walked me through that painful process, I wouldn't be writing this book to help you.

So let me ask you…

- If you're being truly honest with yourself, is there a fear of getting hurt again hiding deep inside?
- Do you feel unworthy of real love on some level?
- Are you more in love with the idea of a Hollywood style happily ever after than with the reality of a healthy, God-honoring relationship?

And here's a harder question:

How many good men have been repelled because, deep down, you weren't emotionally available either?

When Fantasy Masquerades as Love

Let's look at some real-life examples of falling for fantasy instead of reality.

Monica's Story

Monica, a sweet and thoughtful woman with big hazel eyes, had always adored Italian culture. She studied abroad in Italy for a year, learned the language, and dreamed of her own European love story.

While working as a programmer for a tech company in Boston, she met Lorenzo, an actual Italian engineer. Naturally, Monica was drawn to him. He embodied everything she'd dreamed of: romance, charm, sophistication.

They traveled across Europe, and his Italian family welcomed her with open arms. They had a stunning estate and vineyards in Tuscany. Monica felt adored, showered with affection, gifts, and validation.

Lorenzo's family gave her the sense of love and acceptance she had long craved. The attention filled a quiet but powerful emotional void. She was enamored, not just with Lorenzo, but with the fantasy.

But here's what happened next. Monica started noticing things, small red flags.

Lorenzo had a temper. He criticized her, raised his voice often, and blamed her for things that weren't her fault. But Monica dismissed it all as passion. *"He's just a red-hot Italian,"* she told herself.

He started limiting the time she spent with friends and family. When she called out his behavior, he gaslighted her. Somehow, she always ended up being the one apologizing.

Friends warned her, but she ignored them. She didn't want to wake up from the romantic dream. She married him anyway, and they had three children.

Over time, the emotional abuse escalated. The man she once adored now controlled her every move, used his temper to dominate, and eventually betrayed her with serial infidelity. She finally filed for divorce, but not before years of heartbreak, confusion, and soul-weariness.

Fantasy is Seductive, but Reality Sets You Free

Every woman longs to be loved. To be seen. To experience romance. And to live out her version of happily ever after.

It's easy to fall in love with the idea of being in love.

But when we cling to fantasy, we often become blind to reality. We ignore the signs, silence our instincts, and stay stuck in situations that don't serve us, because we're married to the illusion instead of the truth.

If you've been single for a long time, of course loneliness creeps in. That's natural. It's okay to long for love.

But here's what I had to learn the hard way:

It's better to be alone and lonely than married and lonely.

Let that settle in. Because no amount of romance, flowers, or fairy-tale moments can make up for a relationship rooted in fantasy, dishonesty, or dysfunction.

> *FANTASY COMFORTS US FOR A WHILE AS WE AVOID PAIN. BUT WHEN REALITY FINALLY HITS, THOSE FANTASIES SHATTER — AND WE'RE LEFT HOLDING THE TRUTH WE TRIED NOT TO SEE.*
> SOLO TO SOULMATE REFLECTIONS

Healing our souls must come before we meet Mr. Right. The truth is, sometimes we just don't want to see the truth. We avoid facing the pain of our circumstances, and instead, we chase after illusions.

Falling for fantasy is often a form of emotional avoidance, rooted in fear, denial, or an unwillingness to look within.

It's easier to blame others, play the victim, and stay stuck in unhealthy patterns.

In my own relationship with Mr. Wrong, I ignored red flags. I brushed off my intuition. I didn't want to face the truth because it meant confronting uncomfortable realities within myself.

But the key to my freedom began with a simple, yet powerful prayer:

"Lord, hold up a mirror to my heart and help me understand why I made these choices."

And He did.

I gave myself grace to tell the truth, and I allowed God to show me where healing was needed. I did the emotional work. I forgave myself. I learned to love and respect myself again. I let go of shame.

I became what I now call a *"Kingmaker"*, a woman who blesses, supports, and uplifts.

And in time, I met my king. We married, and I've been happily and wonderfully married for over a decade.

Kat The Attorney

Now, let's talk about someone we'll call Kat. She was a successful, attractive corporate attorney with a vibrant social life and a thriving career.

On the surface, Kat had it all, money, influence, and friends. But at 50, she had never been married or had children, and her heart deeply longed for both.

One day, while sitting at a quaint French café, she noticed a very well-known public figure walk in. Their eyes met. She felt an instant connection.

He was magnetic. Charismatic. Captivating. They struck up a long, thoughtful conversation, and she felt something she'd never felt before.

They exchanged social media profiles, but not phone numbers. She never saw him again in person.

Yet... Kat was convinced he was interested in her. She began interpreting his public posts as coded messages meant for her.

In her mind, the reason he hadn't reached out was because of his high-profile status. She believed he had to keep their connection secret to avoid jealousy from other women.

But let's go deeper.

Kat had been an only child. Her parents doted on her. Everything had always revolved around her. And while she was kind and successful, she had unknowingly developed a *WIIFM* mindset, *What's In It For Me?*

She expected others to accommodate her needs, without recognizing how self-centered her expectations had become.

Naturally, emotionally healthy men were repelled.

And after experiencing repeated rejection, she created a fantasy, something she could hold on to, rather than confront the real reason she kept ending up alone.

Instead of examining her patterns or making inner changes, she stayed stuck in the cycle.

The Queen of Delusion

Let's meet *Ann*, a savvy consultant and multi-business owner. One night, she had a dream that a very famous Christian influencer was her future husband.

She followed his public page, attended multiple events where he was speaking, and even traveled to his home state to visit his church.

Ann began connecting with his staff, convinced that befriending them would be her gateway to finally meeting him.

She posted frequently on social media about him, calling him her perfect match, claiming that they were destined to be together. She even referred to herself publicly as the future *"Mrs."* so and so.

Eventually, she moved to his city in another state. In fact, she rented a home on his very street. She went to his church.

All this without ever having had a personal conversation with him.

When it didn't unfold the way she envisioned, she told her followers that an *"evil force"* had blocked the marriage from happening.

So, what could cause a smart, business-savvy woman to fall into such deception?

A deep part of Ann didn't want to be single and have to pay her bills anymore. She was also unwilling to address the root causes of her inner pain.

If we could peek into the crystal ball of her life, we'd see her track record of superhero-deactivator behaviors: shaming, controlling, manipulating, and an unwillingness to examine her own role in past failed relationships.

Ann didn't want a partner to complement her life, she wanted a man who would elevate **her** image and social status. She imagined herself as the wife of a wealthy, influential figure, and her posts reflected that desire.

It wasn't about how she could serve, support, or build a meaningful relationship; it was all about what he could do for her.

WIIFM strikes again.

Both Kat and Ann were deeply intelligent, capable, and accomplished women. But they were also hurting.

And rather than confront their inner wounds, they chose fantasy over reality.

The truth is: when we leave our emotional healing unaddressed, we are far more likely to attract the wrong men, and far less likely to recognize the right ones.

> *IT'S NOT ENOUGH TO BE AT THE RIGHT PLACE AT THE RIGHT TIME. YOU HAVE TO BE THE RIGHT PERSON IN THE RIGHT PLACE AT THE RIGHT TIME.*
> T. HARVE EKER

If you find yourself relating to any of the examples we've explored, take heart. This is excellent news! Why? Because awareness is the first and most powerful key to changing your romantic results.

You are in the wonderful process of becoming the radiant, authentic woman God created you to be. That's something worth celebrating. Way to go, sister!

As we close this chapter, we've uncovered some of the deeper reasons why we sometimes choose not to see the truth, because seeing it means we must confront something within ourselves.

But now, with your growing self-awareness and willingness to look inward, you're learning to recognize your own patterns and motivations.

And guess what? With awareness comes discernment.

Clarity and truth are power. And when we embrace them, we step out of confusion and into freedom.

In the next chapter, we'll explore one of the most unexpected yet beautiful tools for understanding men, love, and even yourself, through the art of dance!

But before we go, here are a couple of food-for-thought journal questions to help you reflect and grow even deeper:

Practical Application

What part of you has been (or is still) drawn to the fantasy more than the reality?

Ask the Holy Spirit to gently show you the *"why"* underneath your attraction to someone or something that may not serve your highest good.

Ask yourself, *"Am I chasing a man, or what I believe having him will say about me?"*

(For example: *"status", "security", "success"* or *even "I finally made it."*)

Write down some inner secret motives or inner lies that come to mind.

_____

_____

_____

_____

If I let go of the dream of what *"could be"* with him, and looked only at who he truly is right now, would I still want this relationship?

_____

_____

_____

_____

Did I hold on to any fantasy beliefs that caused me to overlook red flags or unhealthy behaviors?

(What deeper need was I hoping that fantasy would fulfill, love, safety, validation, status, financial security, etc.?)

_____

_____

_____

_____

Heart Work Assignment

If you need to grieve the pain of past mistakes, it's okay, give yourself permission to feel it. But don't stay there.

Acknowledge the truth of your choices, extend grace to yourself, and thank God for the wisdom you've gained. This season is your classroom for Mr. Right. Every lesson is shaping you, preparing you to love and be loved in a new, healthy, and God-honoring way.

And guess what? He's out there, and he's praying for you too.

For the next seven days, <u>speak these affirmations aloud</u>, with energy from your belly and joy in your voice. Don't just say them, feel them. Own them. These truth statements will help rewire your thoughts and realign your heart with God's best for you.

Experts say it takes 30 days to change a habit, so why not begin right now?

Daily Declarations of Truth

(Say them with boldness! Remember the Scar Experiment from Chapter Three, The Beautiful You, your words carry power!)

- I choose to walk in truth and give myself grace to grow through my weaknesses.
- I am courageous enough to humble myself and embrace change.
- I attract healthy relationships, and my Mr. Right is excited to find me!
- I am radiant, beautiful, and deeply valuable.
- I love and honor myself.
- I receive every blessing heaven is sending my way.
- I release all *WIIFM* mindsets, love is about giving, not just getting.
- I accept myself as I am and who I'm becoming.
- I let go of unforgiveness and bitterness, they have no place in my future.
- I am joyful, successful, and surrounded by God's goodness.
- God is healing my heart and cleansing my soul!

So, are you ready for something you may have never heard before? Let's step into the rhythm and revelation of the next chapter, where we uncover the secrets of relationship patterns through the art of social dancing!

Heart Reflections

FROM JOANNA

I am so proud of you—truly!

You've leaned into truth and uncovered why fantasy can feel safer than reality and why ignoring red flags can feel easier than facing them. That takes courage… and you're doing it beautifully.

The insights you've gained here won't just transform your love life—they'll help your girlfriends too. Breakthroughs spread.

If you want to share your ah-ha moments, join us in the Solo to Soulmate Sisterhood FB group. We'd love to celebrate with you.

Now get ready… because in the next chapter, I'm giving you one of the most surprising tools that shifted my journey from solo to soulmate.

It revealed truth, brought healing, and opened my eyes to myself, men, and relationships in ways I never expected.

Ready for a funny, eye-opening, transformational experience through the art of social dancing?

Let's step into the secrets of rhythm and revelation.

Chapter Twelve

DECODING HIS DANCE MOVES

> ***DANCE IS THE HIDDEN LANGUAGE OF THE SOUL.***
> MARTHA GRAHAM

I've found this quote to be so true. God often uses the most unexpected tools to teach us our most important lessons. He did this with me on my journey from solo to soulmate.

He used many experiences to reveal truth about myself, about men, and about love. But one of the most surprising tools wasn't a book or a conference, it was ballroom dancing.

What started as a fun way to connect quickly became a form of therapy. The dance floor exposed hidden fears, insecurities, and my former need to control.

Even more eye-opening?

It revealed how men function in relationships, how they approach leadership, areas they may need healing in, and how they communicate, build trust, and connect.

In this chapter, I'll share how those simple moments on the dance floor taught me profound lessons about masculine and feminine dynamics, surrender, and trust. You may never look at relationships the same way again.

Let's begin with a few heart-check questions:

- How do you feel about allowing a man to lead?

- How do you handle mistakes made by others? Does this mirror how you manage conflict in relationships?
- Have you ever tried social dance lessons or group classes? If not, are you willing to step out of your comfort zone? Why or why not?

In the **WIIFM Syndrome** chapter, we explored how media and culture often shape our views on gender roles, frequently reinforcing harmful stereotypes like *"You don't need a man,"* *"You can outdo him,"* or *"Men are inept."*

Like many women, I bought into that programming. Sadly, when a gentleman offered to open the door for me, I'd politely decline: *"That's okay, I can do it myself."* If he pulled out my chair, I'd quickly say, *"You don't have to do that."*

As we reflected in *The Beautiful You* chapter, you can now see how not accepting a gift or kind gesture is rejecting the gift of being honored.

Singleness, especially when it lasts longer than expected, can deepen our independence. We become used to doing everything alone.

But self-sufficiency, when combined with media messages, can disconnect us from the feminine parts of ourselves that were created to receive and be cherished.

With that said, let's dive into the fabulous world of ballroom dancing.

With my dear friend and business coach, Terry Johnston, this chapter reflects the shared insights we gained through our parallel ballroom dancing journeys.

Terry's life is as inspiring as her dance steps. A single mom who raised two daughters, a military veteran (2nd Lieutenant in the Army), a terminal cancer survivor (now cancer-free for 30 years thanks to natural therapies), and a thriving businesswoman and grandmother, Terry is a force of faith, resilience, and wisdom.

After 30 years of singleness, she finally met a man who *"deserved her,"* in her words. I had the honor of playing a part in bringing them together. An avid ballroom dancer, Terry, has helped enrich the relationship revelations in this chapter.

Together, we've seen how dancing with a man reveals far more than footwork. It can offer powerful clues into his personality, communication style, leadership tendencies, and even emotional health.

Let me start with a story you'll never forget.

Meet Mr. Machismo

Picture a macho Spaniard with slicked-back, jet black hair. His thick mustache, with its tips curling upwards, was reminiscent of Inigo Montoya from the classic movie, *The Princess Bride.* His deep Spanish accent rolled through the room as he passionately explained the art of the tango to the class.

His outfit screamed charisma, a loud, boldly patterned shirt with the top buttons daringly undone, revealing a heavy gold chain resting against a spray-tanned, freshly shaved chest.

Tight black dance pants showcased his impeccable dancer's posture, as if he'd stepped right out of a telenovela. His dramatic appearance was as unforgettable as his sweeping hand gestures and theatrical dance instructions.

In my mind, I was already laughing, convinced he was a walking movie character. He was, *"explaining the art of tango"* and needed a volunteer. Then, to my absolute horror, he chose ME, out of everyone in the class, to demonstrate the roles of the man and woman in the tango.

I froze. *No. No way. I am not dancing with Señor Movie Star!* But it was almost as if he could read my thoughts. His eyes twinkled, and with a knowing smile he said, *"Joanna, please… come, come and help me teach the class."*

Sweat beaded on my forehead as I tried to follow his lead. But I kept trying to take over, pushing against his direction, causing us both to step on each other's feet. Patient at first, then he finally stopped and exclaimed:

"Stop, stop, stop! You must let go of this controlling and fear. I am the picture frame; you are the picture! Allow me to guide you and help you shine inside the frame."

Time. Stood. Still.

God dropped a revelation into my heart: It's okay to shine, be feminine, and allow a good man to lead. But I had to learn to trust the right partner.

Sensing my internal shift, Mr. Machismo added, *"Joanna, look at me. This is my space, and that is your space. Keep your arms firm and let me hold you. Nooo spaghetti arms! Look into my eyes, and I'll help you glide."*

I took a deep breath. I let go. And I allowed him to lead.

It was a defining moment in my life. His metaphor changed everything. Not just how I approached dance, but how I began to approach life, love, and partnership.

Ready to learn the art of decoding his dance moves? Read on!

Men's Dance Styles and What They Signal

Mr. Two Left Feet

He is often shy or inexperienced, and his awkwardness can be quite endearing, demonstrating a willingness to step out of his comfort zone. This also shows a sense of adventure to try something new. He may not know what he's doing yet, but his eagerness to learn shows that he's coachable.

This also indicates he's aware of his weaknesses and is actively trying to improve by taking classes. He represents potential, someone who, despite discomfort, is willing to try new things, showcasing his adventurous spirit.

Sometimes Mr. Two Left feet, although willing to learn to dance, has a mental block he either doesn't know how to work through or is unwilling to work through it. He is content to stay in that space.

Meet Romeo

Let's take the case of Terry's acquaintance, whom we'll call Romeo. Romeo was a strikingly handsome and charismatic Italian man who captured the attention of many women. He was known for his fun-loving nature and generosity.

However, the social dancing revealed a surprising area of weakness in him. Every Saturday night at the dance, Romeo persisted with dance lessons, week after week, month after month, year after year.

After years of taking dance lessons, he just couldn't get the dance moves. It was like he had two permanent left feet. Terry, an experienced ballroom dancer, would try to work with him, but after a while she felt like his mommy and instructor. She would have to tell him exactly what to do.

Over time, Terry began to dread Romeo's invitations to dance. His charm and good looks no longer compensated for the exhausting effort of laboriously guiding him through each step. Dancing with Romeo felt less like a partnership and more like a chore. Realizing that she needed a partner who could match her step for step rather than one who required constant coaching, Terry concluded that a relationship with Romeo would be too one-sided to work for her.

What's very interesting is that he ended up marrying a controlling and dominating woman, who controls every aspect of the relationship. She tells him when to sit, when to stand, how to dance, what he gets to do, etc.

The Whirlwind Wooer

This dancer loves to spin and dazzle, often with so much enthusiasm that he might accidentally send you spinning into a wall if he loses grip. While his lively spirit and creativity can light up the dance floor, his penchant for being the center of attention needs to be tempered with greater awareness of his partner.

If he ignores gentle guidance on improving his dance etiquette, it may signal a deeper issue of not listening in a relationship, which is a red flag. However, if he's open to feedback and adjusts his approach to meet your needs, he can shine and help you shine. This shows that he has the potential to be a great partner both on and off the dance floor.

I met the whirlwind wooer at a dance in San Francisco. He was handsome, charming with a great energy about him. He was enthusiastically swirling and twirling me around until he accidentally let go of my hand and sent me spinning into the post. Can you say OUCH?!

He apologized profusely, figured out what he needed to do better and then spun me effortlessly around the dance floor from that point forward. He always made sure he had a firm, protective grip. He's an example of the Whirlwind Wooer who was a good Mr. Potential because he was willing to correct himself and adjust.

Mr. Limp Arms

This dancer's lack of assertiveness and decisiveness often mirrors passivity in relationships and a possible lack of confidence. He's adventuresome and is practicing courage because he's taking dance classes and stepping out of his comfort zone. However, if he's not actively working on his self-confidence, he might struggle to lead in a partnership and life.

His limp grip and hesitant moves suggest a fear of stepping out of the box, making decisions and potentially being one who avoids conflict. This is especially problematic if he has a domineering mother or ex-wife, as he may struggle to support you during family disagreements.

Terry experienced Mr. Limp Arms firsthand at a singles ballroom dance. At this class, the women were instructed to line up and the men were instructed to choose a partner.

As the only 6ft blonde left in the lineup of women, she was reluctantly chosen by Mr. Limp Arms, who was visibly intimidated by her height. As the music began, he froze, his grip was weak and uncertain. He was Mr. Limp Arms.

She had to nudge him to start dancing after the music started. Despite the growing congestion on the dance floor, he continued at full speed ahead, unresponsive to Terry's subtle cues to avoid collision. Unable to decide to stop dancing, turn left or right, he inevitably backed her straight into a cement beam. Her head bounced off the concrete pillar.

Stunned and in pain, Terry asked why he didn't stop or turn. All he could do was stare at her and confess he simply couldn't decide what to do. Initially furious, her frustration softened to compassion as she realized his past experiences might have left him a broken man who was berated in life.

This incident highlighted a critical moment for both: an opportunity for Terry to offer grace, realize he was not relationship material and a wake-up call for him to consider how he navigates challenges, not just on the dance floor but in life.

The Dominator

He leads with a force that's more overbearing than guiding, transforming a simple dance into an intense test of endurance. His style involves complicated moves without considering whether you're ready for them, and he quickly shows frustration if you can't keep up. This heavy-handed approach suggests he might be controlling, domineering and possessive in a relationship.

While it's great to have a partner who takes charge and provides protection, his inability to adapt when things don't go as planned could leave you feeling overwhelmed rather than supported.

Dominators are natural leaders, but the best leaders also know how to listen and adjust. If he can't balance his strong leadership with flexibility and empathy, you might feel like you're trapped in a prison partnership.

At a grand ballroom, Mr. Dominator invited Terry for a dance. Quickly, she found herself in an uncomfortably tight hold. He had an iron-clad grip on her. Because of the excessively tight lock, along with the stiff stance he held her in, she was unable to discern his leading. This left her moving in the opposite direction to his intentions, which only fueled his anger.

He blamed her for trying to lead and showed no willingness to listen or adapt to the overly tight grip he had on her. Can you imagine living with someone like that? A definite red flag. Unsurprisingly, he never asked her to dance again, despite frequent encounters at other dances.

I have a saying that, *"Rejection is God's protection."*

The Showman

He's similar to the Performer, but dances to impress, not to connect, often leaving his partner as merely a backdrop to his brilliant dance display. This kind of dancer is all about himself. He loves to be the center of attention and would most likely feel insecure by your success. He's charming, knows how to make you look good, but ultimately, it's all about his performance.

At a glamorous dance studio lined with mirrors and beautiful crystal chandeliers, Terry was swept off her feet by Mr. Showman, a dancer as handsome as he was skilled. They glided and spun like Ginger Rogers and Fred Astaire. It felt like a dream; he knew exactly how to make her shine on the dance floor.

Yet, despite his perfect moves, there was no real connection, every chance he got, he admired his own reflection in the mirrors, bedazzled by himself, never once meeting her eyes.

He was clearly the star of his show, with a role reversal of the picture frame. He was the picture, and Terry was the picture frame. While dancing with him could have been a romantic fairy tale, his self-focus made it clear that a true partnership was off the table. Would she want a life with someone who couldn't truly see her? Absolutely not.

The Gallant Guider

The ideal dance partner. He leads confidently yet gently, adapting his moves to match his partner's skill level. His style reflects a balanced approach to relationships, characterized by respect, attentiveness, and support. He's patient when you make a mistake and knows how to lead.

One of the most memorable dancers I experienced during my single years was at a beautiful ballroom dance hall overlooking the water in San Diego.

A handsome, Patrick Swayze (from the classic movie Dirty Dancing) looking man approached me and asked me to dance. He had captivating eyes, a sexy smile, was strong and chiseled, yet kind, assertive, confident but not arrogant. The lights glimmered as he glided and twirled me around the dance floor, making it effortless to dance. His grip was firm and protective, not tight and controlling.

I knew he wasn't going to let me go and send me hurling into a beam or wall. He kept eye contact with me as we gracefully moved together across the floor.

We moved as one, making me *the picture inside the picture frame.* He was a foreshadowing of the qualities of my husband (Dr. David) that God had for me.

What About Your Dance Style?

Just as we decode his steps, it's time to decode yours.

Are you trying to lead when you're meant to follow? Are you controlling out of fear, or are you learning to trust, to respond, and to be cherished?

My former dance style was to take control. I didn't trust the man to lead, and we ended up stepping on each other's toes. But once I let go, everything changed.

> *A WOMAN'S TRUE POWER IS NOT IN HOW SHE LEADS THE DANCE, BUT IN HOW GRACEFULLY SHE ALLOWS HERSELF TO BE LED.*
> ANONYMOUS

Let's take a deeper dive into which dance style you resonate with, especially if you've had past social or ballroom dance experiences. And if you've never tried ballroom dancing before, I highly recommend it, for so many reasons.

- If you're shy, it helps you break out of your shell.
- If you struggle with control, it can gently nudge you toward balance by practicing how to let a man lead.
- If you're creative, it invites you to collaborate, learning how to bring someone else into the rhythm of your expression.

Dance helps you find balance in both movement and relationship.

We'd love to hear your thoughts on this chapter! Join the conversation on the Solo to Soulmate Sisterhood Facebook page. It's a safe and supportive space filled with women who contrast and complete each other, we don't compete or compare. We lift one another up.

Now let's take a look at what your dance style might be saying to the men you dance and do life with.

Women's Dance Styles & What They Signal to Men

The Controller

She often tries to lead the dance, signaling a tendency to take charge in relationships. This may reflect challenges with trust, fear of vulnerability, or deep-seated insecurities about letting go of control.

The Follower

She flows naturally with her partner's lead, showing trust and adaptability. While this is beautiful, she must be mindful of keeping healthy boundaries and not losing her voice or identity in the relationship.

The Improviser

She adds flair and spontaneity, suggesting independence and creativity. While this is exciting, she may need to work on aligning her rhythm with her partner's, remembering that she is the picture and he is the frame.

The Hesitant

Timid and unsure on the dance floor, she may struggle with confidence in relationships too. It's important that she strengthens her self-worth, as we explored in Chapter Two, The Beautiful You.

The Enthusiast

Full of energy and ready to try new moves, she brings passion and zest to the floor. But sometimes, this excitement can mask deeper fears around trust and emotional intimacy. She may need to focus on building deeper connections that go beyond the initial spark.

Ultimately, the goal is learning how to trust, when to lead, and when to follow.

Whether on the dance floor or in life, learning to move in harmony with another person takes humility, courage, and adaptability.

I discovered that dance mirrors our romantic interactions. It teaches us about timing, trust, compromise, and the beauty of giving and receiving grace in every misstep.

And friend, hear me when I say: The best is yet to come for you.

Are You Ready to Define Mr. Right and Discover the SECRET KEY to Calling Him In?

You don't want to miss the next chapter! I'm so proud of you. You are in the beautiful process of transformation. Get ready to start calling in the love that's been waiting for you.

Homework Assignment

This next assignment is both fun and eye-opening and will give you insight into how your dance style mirrors your relationship patterns.

Here's what to do:

Take a ballroom dance class (or classes) and stay for the social dance afterward. Then, reflect and journal your experience.

Practical Application

Observations

- What did you notice about yourself on the dance floor?
- Were you leading, following, hesitating, improvising, or, enthusiastically engaging?
- What emotions came up for you?
- What did you notice about your dance partners?

Journal Insights

Questions to Consider:

- How did I feel when my partner led the dance? Did I follow seamlessly?
- Did I feel the urge to take control? Why?
- How did I react to my partner's suggestions or steps?

Food for Thought Options

- Ask your dance partner(s) for feedback on your dancing interaction.
- Gather insights into how your dance style might come across to others.
- Reflect on your past or current relationships.
- Which dance style do I most resonate with in my romantic relationships?
- How might these behaviors be affecting my relationship dynamics?
- Are there any consistent issues or feedback I've received from partners that align with my dance style?

Setting Intentions for Adjustments

Based on your insights, set specific intentions on how you can adjust your dance and relationship styles.

Examples:

- If you're a Controller, practice letting your partner lead more often to build trust.
- If you're a Follower, work on asserting your needs and maintaining boundaries.
- If you're an Improviser, ensure your creativity supports mutual goals in the relationship.
- If you're Hesitant, seek ways to boost your confidence, possibly through solo dance lessons or assertiveness training.
- If you're an Enthusiast, focus on deepening emotional connections beyond the initial excitement.

Practice and Evaluate Progress

Continue attending dance sessions while consciously working on your intentions.

Note benchmarks, your *"ah-hahs"* and insight. Celebrate all your efforts!! Practice new behaviors in a low-stakes environment and reflect on any changes in how you feel and interact.

Great job!! Are you ready to rewrite your love story?! Let's do this in the next chapter!

Chapter Thirteen

RE-WRITING YOUR LOVE STORY

> *YOU CAN'T GO BACK AND CHANGE THE BEGINNING,*
> *BUT YOU CAN START WHERE YOU ARE AND CHANGE*
> *THE ENDING.*
> C.S LEWIS

CONGRATULATIONS, WE'RE JUST ABOUT THERE!

Take a deep breath and take pride in how far you've come. You are becoming the fabulous, upgraded version of yourself! You've done the heart work, the inner work, and the spiritual work.

You've shown up with strength, beauty, vulnerability, and courage. That, my friend, takes guts. Welcome to the Courage Club!

You're no longer repeating old patterns, you're reshaping your destiny. You've begun to speak life, form new beliefs, and create space for the kind of love that honors who you truly are.

Remember:

- Words build or destroy.
- Thoughts shape beliefs.
- Beliefs create patterns.

And patterns determine your outcomes.

So, as we prepare to step into the final chapter, let's pause to reflect. This recap will reinforce the powerful truths you've learned, while also equipping you with **bonus tools** like the: *Superhero Deactivators Checklist, Queenly Behavior Guide, and a Dating Red Flag Reference Sheet.*

If someone had handed me this book earlier in my journey, I truly believe it could've saved me from a lot of heartache and detours. But praise God, he works all things together for good for those who love Him and are called according to His purpose (Romans 8:28).

With Him, all things are possible.

Let's dive into what we've covered:

Chapter One: The WIIFM Syndrome

We explored the two sides of the WIIFM *(What's In It For Me?)* mindset:

Healthy WIIFM: Sets healthy boundaries, practices mutual giving, and fosters servant-hearted relationships.

Unhealthy WIIFM: Focuses on self-gratification and entitlement, leading to disappointment and emotional disconnection.

We also unmasked the influence of Hollywood scripts and cultural programming, the subtle ways media misrepresents both men and women. Recognizing those false narratives empowers you to rewrite your own love story based on truth and wholeness.

Chapter Two: The Superhero Deactivators

This chapter unpacked the silent saboteurs; the ways women unknowingly deactivate a good man's desire to show up and serve.

You learned:

How words, tone, and reactions either build or break connection.

Why a good man is wired to protect, provide, and pursue, and how the reflection you hold up to him (your Man Mirror) shapes how he sees himself.

"You're not good enough." "You're doing it wrong." "I don't need you."

These silent messages chip away at confidence.

But when you reflect honor, belief, and respect? He rises.

Chapter Three: The Beautiful You

We dove deep into healing your view of self and receiving the love you deserve.

You discovered:

- **The Power of Agreement**: Aligning with truth over lies.
- **The Power of Words:** Speaking life into yourself and others.
- **The Power of Receiving:** Learning to graciously receive love, help, and kindness.
- **The Power of Forgiveness:** Releasing yourself from past mistakes.
- **The Scar Experiment** revealed how self-perception shapes how others respond to us. When you believe you're beautiful and worthy, the world begins to agree.

Chapter Four: The Hidden Love Superpower

We explored the powerful relationship changer: Emotional Intelligence (EQ). Growing in your EQ means becoming aware of triggers and learning how to manage your responses differently.

You learned:

How to avoid damaging phrases like *"You always," "You never,"* or *"You should"*

The importance of *Clear Speak* vs. *Code Speak*, because clarity is kindness.

That even the most brilliant women can struggle in love without emotional maturity.

The good news? *EQ* is a skill, and you've already started developing it.

Chapter Five: The Kingmaker vs. The Man-Breaker

A powerful reminder: You hold influence.

You can either: Be a Kingmaker, who inspires, uplifts, and honors. Or become a Man-Breaker, who criticizes, controls, complains and erodes.

Just like the queen in chess, your role isn't to dominate, it's to protect, empower, and speak life.

Remember: To a good man, no voice matters more than yours.

Chapter Six: The Reverse Trainer

Here, we learned how difficulty in receiving love and kindness leads to unintentional rejection.

By brushing off compliments, declining help, or minimizing gifts, the Reverse Trainer teaches others that their efforts aren't welcome. The result? Disconnection.

Often rooted in a victim mindset, this behavior blocks intimacy and trust.

The solution? Own your worth. Open your heart. And allow love in.

Chapter Seven: The Disguised Doormat

You might look powerful on the outside, but if you lose yourself in relationships, constantly say yes, and sacrifice your needs, you're playing small.

This chapter exposed the *Yes Syndrome* and the consequences of over-accommodating.

Healthy love requires balance, boundaries, and self-respect.

Chapter Eight: The Queen of Chaos

In this chapter, we tackled the tendency to overshare to much drama too soon, a pattern that drives emotionally healthy men away.

The Queen of Chaos confuses intensity with intimacy, often using her personal storms to connect rather than heal.

Truth? Peace is powerful.

And the right man is drawn not to chaos, but to confidence and calm.

Chapter Nine: The Director

Aka, the *"Backseat Driver"* in dating.

Directors often feel the need to control everything, from how their man parks to how he prays.

But behind control is often a fear of letting go, or a subconscious desire to manage a project instead of being in a partnership.

Letting go of the reins, trusting the process, and allowing a man to lead in his own way are keys to building trust and connection.

Chapter Ten: The One Upper

This dynamic is subtle but destructive.

The One-Upper competes with her man, one-upping his stories, diminishing his opinions, and constantly needing to be *"right."*

This kills connection and creates shame in the relationship.

True love isn't competitive, it's collaborative. And humility, not superiority, builds intimacy.

Chapter Eleven: The Fantasizer

The Fantasizer falls in love with fantasy: potential, possibility, or rescue, not reality.

This woman clings to illusions to fill loneliness or chase a fairytale. She overlooks red flags and ignores her intuition in favor of the dream.

But you learned: Real love is grounded in truth.

And truth is the foundation for the love God designed for you.

Final Reflection

Through each chapter, you've taken brave steps, by taking responsibility for your actions and heart.

You now understand the important steps to becoming the beautiful, vibrant, healthy version of yourself to attract Mr. Right.

You're aware of the importance of maintaining your identity, such as maintaining your own interests, hobbies, and friends throughout your relationship.

> *YOU ARE ALTOGETHER BEAUTIFUL, MY DARLING;*
> *THERE IS NO FLAW IN YOU.*
> SONG OF SONGS 4:7 (NIV)

As we've discussed throughout this journey, awareness is the foundation of real and lasting change. I personally live by the principles I've shared with you, and they are the reason my marriage to David continues to thrive. **These tools work because they are rooted in truth, grace, and intentional action.**

If we model what healthy, successful relationships look like, and put those practices into motion, we can experience the same success.

To support your transformation even further, I've included a quick reference checklist of *Superhero Deactivator Behaviors* (the ones we want to avoid) and *Queenly Behaviors* (that inspire and encourage the good man you're praying for).

Following that, you'll also find a bonus Dating Red Flag Checklist to guide you through your dating journey with discernment and confidence.

Good practice produces good results. Bad practice reinforces bad results.

The more you practice what you've learned, the more natural these heart habits become, and the closer you step toward attracting and sustaining a God-honoring, healthy relationship.

We want to avoid these common behaviors that shut down a man's inner superhero.

Ready for the checklists? Here we go!

Superhero Deactivator Checklist

- Shaming your man, whether in private or public, for his mistakes or shortcomings.
- Consistently directing, instructing, or correcting him about how to act, dress, or think.
- Becoming overly needy, insecure, or jealous, expecting him to complete you or fill your emotional gaps.
- Rejecting compliments, gifts, or gestures, sending the message that his efforts aren't valued.
- Talking excessively about yourself or interrupting him, while failing to validate his thoughts and emotions.
- Treating him like a *"project"* to fix or manage, rather than a partner to support and respect.
- Criticizing, correcting, or redoing his efforts. If he feels he can never win, he'll stop trying.
- Competing with him, one upping, refusing to apologize, or always needing to be right.
- Bringing chaos or drama into the relationship and emotionally dumping on him.
- Playing the victim and avoiding responsibility for how your words and actions affect him.
- Using a snarky or accusatory tone, assuming the worst rather than believing the best.
- Falling into *Yes* Syndrome, losing your identity and revolving your life around him.
- Paying for everything and assuming the financial lead if he isn't stepping up, if he can't care for himself, he's not ready for you.
- Expecting and assuming him to read your mind and getting angry when he doesn't understand your unspoken needs.
- Don't redo his work or tell him to do it your way.

Queenly Behaviors that Inspire the Good King

Cultivate these empowering habits to nurture a life-giving connection:

- Receive honest compliments with a smile and a simple "thank you."
- Ask about his dreams, goals, and interests. Listen intentionally and affirm his answers.
- Be intentional about offering genuine compliments. If you're not currently dating, practice on friends or service workers, gratitude is a heart posture.
- Maintain healthy personal boundaries around your time, energy, finances, and emotions.
- Create a safe space for vulnerability, where he feels seen, heard, and respected without fear of judgment.
- Appreciate his efforts, big or small. Gratitude fuels more goodness.
- Speak well of him both publicly and privately. Example: *"You look so handsome in that color,"* or *"You did a great job with"*
- Smile! A woman who walks into a room with warmth and light in her countenance is unforgettable.
- Don't dictate, ask before offering advice. If he says no, honor that boundary.
- Let him serve you: open doors, carry things, offer help. Say thank you and affirm his effort, he'll want to do more.
- When discussing issues, assume the best: *"I know this wasn't intentional"* or *"You may not have realized"* rather than *"You always"* or *"You never"*
- Celebrate even the little things, like doing the dishes. Tell him it's sexy, he'll light up.

- Refrain from acting as his advice coach. He doesn't need a mother; he needs a partner.
- Speak life over him. Remind him of his strengths and express belief in his ability to rise.
- Hold up the Man Mirror, one of honor, respect, and faith in him. Your belief in him can shape how he sees himself.

Learning new habits takes time, but consistency leads to transformation. Revisit these lists often. Keep practicing the daily heart work. Let your thoughts, words, and actions align with the woman you're becoming.

You are now fully positioned emotionally, spiritually, and relationally, to attract a good man who is ready to honor, cherish, and walk beside you in purpose and partnership.

They have also positioned you to maintain a strong, healthy relationship when he comes along.

As you continue growing and transforming, you'll start to notice something beautiful: healthy, emotionally grounded men will begin to gravitate toward you.

Testimony: Let me share a real-life story from one of my coaching clients.

She discovered that she had been living as a Disguised Doormat, married to a very self-absorbed man. The marriage didn't last. It ended in divorce, and she found herself raising three kids alone.

But here's the redemptive part.

As she courageously began her journey of awareness, healing, forgiveness, and transformation, I watched her blossom. She committed to the practical work in this book, honestly, actively, and consistently. I couldn't be prouder of her.

And what happened next?

She attracted a wonderful man we'll call Ray. He treats her like the queen she now knows she is, because she first learned to respect herself and to honor him in return. Ray is kind, generous, attentive, and deeply loving in ways she had never experienced before.

So what changed? She did.

She became coachable. She did the work. She changed her internal world, and her external world followed.

During her journey to meeting Ray, she encountered a few other Mr. Potentials, men she would have fallen for in her past, especially the charming *"bad boys."* But now that she had grown into a healthier place emotionally and spiritually, she recognized the red flags and didn't engage. Her new awareness gave her the power to walk away with peace.

And that's the key...

Awareness, not fear, is your greatest protector.

When you're healed and whole, you no longer get caught in the wash, rinse, repeat cycle of attracting the wrong man. Instead, you start identifying potential issues early, and you move forward in freedom, not fear.

I remember facing this fear myself. After my own divorce from Mr. Wrong, one of my biggest concerns was falling into the same patterns and choosing another man who wasn't right for me.

But as I healed and aligned with God's truth, I became more confident, clear, and whole. I began recognizing red flags almost instantly. And when I spotted them, I passed without drama or heartbreak.

That kind of clarity and peace is possible for you too.

So, let's dive into a powerful BONUS section: *Online and In-Person Dating Red Flags Checklists.* If I had known about these back then, I could have saved myself a lot of heartache with my ex-Mr. Wrong.

BONUS: Online Dating Red Flags Checklist

- Too Good to Be True: Their profile looks like a movie star highlight reel and reads like a romance novel.
- No Digital Footprint: No social media, no traceable online presence, could indicate a fake identity.
- Rush to Get Personal: They want your phone number or private info within minutes of chatting.
- Love Bombing Early: Big declarations of love, "soulmate" talk, or emotional intensity within days or weeks.
- Avoiding Video or In-Person Meetings: Constant excuses, scheduling conflicts, or camera "issues."
- Inconsistent Stories: Changing details about their job, location, or background.
- Asks for Money or Gifts: Any request for financial help, no matter how small, is a **hard no.**
- Always in a Distant Location: Claims to be overseas, on deployment, or constantly traveling with no proof.
- Excessively Secretive: Dodges basic questions about their life, job, or family.
- Lots of Sob Stories: A trail of tragic tales designed to hook your sympathy.
- Hot and Cold Communication: Ghosts you, then suddenly floods your inbox.
- Vague Profile or Stock Photos: Few details, blurry photos, or images that look suspiciously professional.

In-Person Dating Red Flags Checklist

- Disrespects Boundaries: Pushes physical or emotional limits, ignores your clear "no."
- Financial Dependence: Asks you to pay for things, co-sign loans, give him money or *"help"* with his rent or bills.
- Controlling Tendencies: Tells you what to wear, who to talk to, or how to act.
- Early Love Bombing: Excessive flattery, over-the-top romance, or future talk too soon.
- Anger Issue or Aggression Reaction: Road rage, yelling over minor issues, or explosive temper.
- Overly Critical or Negative: Constant criticism, especially of you, past partners, or strangers.
- Extreme Jealousy: Suspicious of your interactions, even early on.
- Gaslighting: Causes you to question your reality or emotions. Says things like, *"You're too sensitive"* or *"I was just joking."*
- Secretive About the Past: Won't share basic information about family or former relationships.
- Inconsistent Behavior: One day hot, the next day cold. Emotionally unreliable.
- Substance Abuse: Regular drinking, drug use, or using substances to escape reality.
- Unreliable or Flaky: Constantly late, cancels often, or disappears without explanation.
- Rude to Others: Treats waitstaff or service workers poorly.
- Disregards Your Comfort: Pressures you sexually or emotionally, even after you say no.
- Keeps You a Secret: Doesn't introduce you to friends or family, or hides the relationship.

- Obsessed with Exes: Talks too much about a former partner, either love or hate.
- Blame Shifter: Plays the victim in every story, never takes ownership of past problems.

Eye opening, right?

But here's something critical I want you to remember:

Don't get stuck in fear. Whatever you focus on, you attract.

If you live in fear of picking the wrong man, you'll remain stuck in patterns that reflect that fear. But if you focus on truth, growth, and discernment, you'll attract what aligns with your healed heart.

I used to be paralyzed by the fear of repeating past mistakes. But as I grew in God's truth and became more aligned with my identity, I realized:

I'm not the same woman who once chose Mr. Wrong, so I won't be drawn to him again.

Instead, I recognized red flags instantly and walked away with confidence and clarity.

Every chapter you've completed so far has laid a foundation. You've discovered blind spots, challenged limiting beliefs, and started rewiring your relationship patterns for the better.

You've grown more self-aware. You're stronger, wiser, and more radiant than ever.

The definition of a princess is a woman who is strong, courageous, and walks in dominion.

And by that definition, you are absolutely a princess of the King of Heaven.

Now comes the next powerful step: defining who Mr. Right truly is, and how to align with the kind of relationship you desire.

In the next chapter, we'll go deep into your values, alignment, and relationship non-negotiables. Most women skip this step, but not you. You're ready to attract with clarity and connect with purpose.

You're about to define Mr. Right, and step boldly into your destiny.

Chapter Fourteen

DEFINING MR. RIGHT!

> *FINDING THE RIGHT MAN ISN'T ABOUT HOW*
> *PERFECT HE IS, BUT HOW PERFECT HE IS FOR YOU.*
> *IT'S ABOUT SEEING AN IMPERFECT PERSON,*
> *RECOGNIZING HOW HIS STRENGTHS AND FLAWS*
> *MAKE YOU GROW.*
> ANONYMOUS

Great job transforming yourself, and ultimately your life, to attract the soulmate God has for you!

I am so proud of you. This final chapter is the exclamation point of everything we've been building toward.

Now, we're going to dive into the qualities you desire in a partner and begin to visualize the kind of relationship you want. With the foundation stones and skills you've laid throughout this journey, you are now ready to start calling in the one!

Are you ready for what might just be the most fun chapter of the book?

Let's go!

Why Is It Important to Define Mr. Right?

Because you're in the process of shedding the *"old wineskin"* to make room for the "new wineskin."

There's a profound parable in the New Testament that beautifully illustrates this: *You cannot pour new wine into old wineskins.*

Why? Because the new wine, still fermenting and expanding, would burst the old, brittle wineskins, which are no longer flexible enough to hold it.

This is a powerful metaphor for what you're experiencing.

The new wine represents fresh ideas, renewed self-worth, and new beginnings. The old wineskin symbolizes outdated mindsets, limiting beliefs, and past patterns that no longer serve you.

You've spent this journey peeling away the old wineskin, old ways of thinking, reacting, and relating, and in its place, you've received new wine: new tools, mindset shifts, emotional maturity, and spiritual wisdom.

This book has been preparing your heart and your habits for the kind of love story God wants to write with you and Mr. Right.

Choosing the right partner isn't about finding perfection, it's about identifying values, vision, and character that align with your purpose and heart.

That starts by knowing yourself, your values, and what you truly desire in a partner and in a relationship.

So now, we're going to walk through a process that helps you define the kind of man you want to invite into your life. This clarity will not only sharpen your discernment but will also help you recognize the right relationship when it comes.

(And yes, in my coaching program we go deeper into this step together!)

Creating Your Love Vision

Write it. Speak it. Believe it. Receive it!

Before we dive into listing the qualities you want in a soulmate, I invite you to visualize the relationship you desire.

Close your eyes and imagine:

- What does your day-to-day life together look like?
- How do you communicate and resolve conflict?
- How do you feel emotionally, spiritually, and physically when you're with him?
- How do you grow together? Laugh together? Pray together?

This step is a powerful combination of dreaming and intentional design.

I highly recommend writing it down and creating a vision board (or even a vision book!) to reinforce what you want to experience. Writing helps clarify your thoughts. Visualizing helps feel it into reality.

Step One: Clearly Define Your Values

Before anything else, we need to get crystal clear on your values, your non-negotiables, and your desires. Most women don't take the time to do this and often end up with less-than-desirable results.

But not you. You're intentional now.

Step Two: Write Your Declarations

Once you've identified your values, you'll write out your declarations, truth-filled, faith-based affirmations about the man you are attracting and the kind of relationship you are creating with him.

This isn't wishful thinking. This is kingdom alignment, partnering with God and declaring what you are ready to receive based on the truth of who you are.

Step Three: Create Your Vision Board

Now it's time to get creative and inspired! Pull out your magazines, scissors, glue, Canva boards, Pinterest, whatever speaks to you, and visually represent your relationship vision.

But before we jump into step three of the vision boarding, let's begin by laying down the most important foundation of defining your values.

As you continue transforming into the best version of yourself, emotionally whole, spiritually grounded, and radiating self-worth, your energy will begin to magnetize the kind of man who is not only looking for you; but also aligned to love you well.

When I became that version of me healed, whole, and confident. I was finally ready to receive my husband, Dr. David. My true knight in shining armor.

And let me just say, he was worth the wait!

As you begin to craft your own version of Mr. Right, don't just think about his surface-level traits (though those can be fun!). Think deeply about the emotional, spiritual, and relational dynamics of the love you want to build.

Food-for-Thought Journaling Prompts

Reflect on and journal about:

- How do you want to communicate and feel emotionally connected?
- What values and lifestyle do you want to share?
- How do you want to support each other in challenges?
- How does he lead, and how do you partner with him?

- What kind of laughter, vision, and faith will you build together?

Quick Caution: Don't Overbuild the Wall

A loving reminder from someone who's walked this path:

No man is perfect. And neither are we.

Be careful not to create an impossible checklist that's rooted in fear, hyper-control, or self-protection. Sometimes, those overly specific lists are really just emotional armor, shields meant to keep us "safe" but that also block love from ever getting in.

(Ask me how I know this!)

Now it's your turn.

Grab your favorite beverage, notebook, and a pen.

Take your time with Step One: *Values and Relationship Clarification.*

This is your love story, be intentional and prayerful about what matters most to you.

When you're ready, move on to Step Two!

Need support or want to bounce around your thoughts?

Join us in the Solo to Soulmate Sisterhood Facebook group! We're here to walk this journey with you.

Values and Relationship Checklist

1. Values Alignment

What principles are non-negotiable in your life?

Honesty?

Kindness?

A heart for God?

Sexual purity before marriage?

Ambition?

Compassion?

A strong work ethic?

Your soulmate doesn't need to be your clone, but he should reflect and respect your core values.

Misaligned values don't just cause disagreements; they quietly fracture intimacy at its foundation.

Ask yourself:

What values do I actually live by, not just admire or aspire to?

_____

_____

_____

_____

_____

_____

_____

_____

_____

_____

_____

_____

_____

_____

_____

_____

_____

_____

_____

_____

_____

_____

_____

_____

_____

_____

_____

2. Emotional Availability

Based on what you learned in Decoding His Dance Moves, let's
explore a key question:

Is your future partner emotionally available?

Is he open-hearted and willing to communicate honestly, even
when it's uncomfortable?

Can he show up vulnerably, sharing his inner world, not just his
accomplishments?

Does he have the capacity to pivot, to adjust, grow, and respond
when the relationship calls for change?

Is he healed or actively healing from his past, or is he still
carrying emotional baggage that he hasn't yet faced?

Ask yourself:

Does he want to be the picture or the picture frame?

In a healthy, God-aligned relationship, he is the frame, strong,
steady, and supportive, while you are the beautiful picture within
it. A man who is emotionally available knows how to hold space
for your heart, your voice, and your needs.

Can you see yourself trusting his leadership, knowing he values your thoughts and takes your perspective seriously?

Another essential trait to look for:

Is he coachable in the small things?

Does he welcome gentle feedback and care about how his actions affect you?

Remember: No one can pour from an empty cup.

An emotionally unavailable man may seem appealing at first, but over time, his inability to connect deeply will create a void that love alone cannot fill.

_____
_____
_____
_____
_____
_____
_____
_____
_____
_____
_____
_____
_____
_____
_____
_____

_____

_____

_____

_____

_____

_____

_____

_____

3. Lifestyle Compatibility

Let's talk about the rhythm of real life.

Do your everyday lives fit together?

Beyond romance and chemistry, daily compatibility matters a lot.

Think about your routines: How do you each like to spend your weekends?

Are you energized by shared activities or do you need regular solo time to recharge?

Are you early risers or night owls?

Is fitness important to you both?

Do you thrive on structure or live for spontaneity?

Even the little things, like whether he leaves socks on the floor or makes the bed, can become daily friction points or opportunities for grace.

Ask yourself:

- Do you want someone adventurous or more laid-back?
- Do you need predictability or love a little unpredictability?

And here's a gentle nudge, if you expect him to be punctual but you're always 15 minutes late, it might be time to realign your own habits.

Compatibility isn't about being exactly the same, it's about learning to dance together in life's everyday rhythm, with mutual respect, understanding, and grace.

_____
_____
_____
_____
_____
_____
_____
_____
_____
_____
_____
_____
_____
_____
_____
_____
_____
_____
_____
_____

4. Intellectual Match

Let's talk about a mind-to-mind connection.

Do you crave deep, meaningful conversations that challenge and inspire you? Or do you find comfort in quiet strength and emotional steadiness?

Think about how your mind works, and what kind of mental and emotional engagement feeds your soul.

Do you want a partner who's highly analytical and loves discussing ideas and strategy? Or are you more drawn to someone who's creative, expressive, and intuitive?

Here's the truth: An intellectual match doesn't require matching degrees or IQs.

It's about mutual curiosity, respect, and a shared desire to grow together, mentally, emotionally, and spiritually.

The best relationships aren't about who knows more, but about how you sharpen and inspire each other to keep learning, dreaming, and becoming.

_____

_____

_____

_____

_____

_____

_____

_____

_____

_____

_____

_____

_____

_____

_____

_____

_____

5. Sense of Humor

So let's reflect:

What kind of humor do you naturally enjoy?

Do you love playful banter? Witty and clever jokes? A little light-hearted teasing? Or maybe you appreciate dry, subtle humor?

Now think about the humor you don't enjoy sarcasm that stings, excessive self-deprecation, or dark humor that feels heavy. These can sometimes reveal what's buried deeper.

Sarcasm, for example, can mask hidden anger.

Excessive self-deprecation might hint at unresolved insecurity.

Dark humor may be a clue to unprocessed emotional pain.

"Out of the abundance of the heart, the mouth speaks." (Luke 6:45)

So ask yourself:

Does his humor uplift you, or subtly tear you down?

Do you laugh together, or does it feel like you're the punchline?

Know the kind of humor that fills your heart with joy and the kind that drains it.

Laughter should bond you, not bruise you.

6. Supportive Nature

Support and encouragement are cornerstones of a thriving, God-centered relationship.

Ask yourself:

How important is it to you that your partner isn't just proud of you, but is truly your biggest fan?

Do you want someone who cheers you on without competition, celebrates your wins with genuine joy, and champions your dreams as if they were his own?

That's what healthy support looks like, and in a soul-aligned relationship, it goes both ways. So pause and reflect:

Am I ready to be that kind of partner, too?

Also consider your personal need for freedom and space. Are you someone who thrives with independence and values autonomy within the relationship?

If so, what does freedom look like for you in the context of a God-honoring marriage?

Can you clearly define it so your future husband can support it, and feel secure in it?

_____

_____

_____

_____

_____

_____

_____

_____

_____

_____

_____

_____

_____

_____

_____

_____

_____

_____

_____

_____

_____

_____

_____

_____

_____

7. Relationship Goals

Does he want marriage? Children? Do you want children? These aren't small questions, they're foundational. Be honest with yourself about what's a deal-breaker, and don't ignore misalignment hoping he'll *"come around."* Start clear. Stay clear.

Does he carry a vision for a Kingdom-purpose partnership, where you serve God together, grow spiritually, and walk in unity both emotionally and practically?

What about his past? If he has an ex or children, what kind of relationship exists there? Can you navigate those dynamics with grace and peace long-term? It's important to consider what your daily life might look like in those situations, not just in theory, but in reality.

And don't forget to look beyond the now. What kind of life do you want to build in the later seasons? Do you both see yourselves traveling, serving in ministry, enjoying shared hobbies, living near family, giving back, or starting something new together?

Marriage isn't just about finding someone to share the present with, it's about building a life that honors God in every season. Make sure the man you're praying in isn't just right for today, but also right for tomorrow.

Be intentional. Be honest. And trust that alignment brings peace, while misalignment, no matter how charming, brings confusion.

_____

_____

_____

_____

_____

_____

_____

_____

_____

_____

_____

_____

_____

_____

_____

_____

_____

_____

8. Spiritual Compatibility

This one's big, non-negotiable, really.

Where is he spiritually? Are you truly equally yoked in your beliefs, convictions, and pursuit of God? Does he live out the values you hold dear? Spiritual compatibility isn't just about attending church or quoting scripture, it's about shared vision, active faith, and alignment in how you both walk with the Lord.

Ask yourself: Is he spiritually leading his own life well? Or are you hoping to *"inspire"* or *"elevate"* him spiritually once you're together? (That, my friend, is called missionary dating, and it's a hard pass.)

Reminder: You can't marry potential. Look for spiritual fruit, not just faith-filled talk. A man who is led by God before marriage is far more likely to lead well in marriage.

If you're dreaming of building a Kingdom marriage, start by choosing someone who's already building his life on Kingdom principles.

_____

_____

_____

_____

_____

_____

_____

_____

_____

_____

_____

_____

_____

_____

_____

_____

_____

_____

_____

_____

_____

_____

_____

_____

_____

9. Sexual Compatibility

Yes, Queen, we're going there. Because this matters.

Sexual compatibility is a crucial part of a thriving, God honoring marriage. And while many shy away from this topic, it's essential to know yourself in this area, your boundaries, desires, needs, and places of healing. When the time is right (and within the context of emotional maturity and commitment), you'll also need to have honest, prayerful conversations with your future Mr. Right.

Ask yourself:

What are my beliefs and boundaries around sex in marriage?

What does healthy sexual connection look like for me?

How often do I desire intimacy, and how important is physical affection to me?

Are there any sexual preferences, expectations, or limitations I need to be upfront about?

Is my future husband walking in healing and full deliverance from past sexual issues, or is he merely abstaining while still struggling in secret?

Here's the truth: sexual mismatch can lead to deep frustration, unmet needs, and disconnection, even in otherwise loving relationships. You both deserve a healthy, joyful, and respectful connection, one that honors God and feels emotionally and physically safe.

I once had a client who didn't enjoy giving or receiving oral sex. Thankfully, her husband didn't either. However, they discussed the topic while dating and BEFORE marriage. Very important. If it hadn't been a match, they wouldn't have gotten married. It wasn't awkward or forced, it was a match. They aligned because they communicated and knew themselves.

You're not looking for perfection, but you are looking for alignment. Don't avoid this conversation. Be prayerful, be honest, and know that your needs matter too.

Welcome Back and Way to Go Doing the Work!

Now that you've defined your values, it's time to speak life into them.

This next step is where we begin turning heart clarity into heart alignment.

Step Two: Ready to Write Your Declarations?

This is more than a journaling exercise. This is a sacred moment, a heart-powered declaration of the kind of love you're calling in. And just as important, it's about choosing to believe that you are worthy of receiving it.

Writing and speaking your declarations daily, with energy, joy, and conviction is one of the most powerful tools you'll use to shape your future. Why? Because your words carry spiritual authority, and your emotions act like a magnet.

What you declare, and the energy you carry behind those words, will either draw life to you or repel it.

If you speak your desires with frustration, fear, or doubt, you're unintentionally reinforcing an energetic blueprint of lack. But when you speak from joy, gratitude, and expectancy? Everything begins to shift.

I'll never forget some of the things I used to say:

- *"I'll never find a man who matches me spiritually."*
- *"Why is it so hard to find a good man?"*
- *"I'll probably be rolling down the aisle in a wheelchair before I finally meet the right one!"*

And I didn't just say those things, I said them with emotion. Sadness, frustration, fear. I unknowingly kept affirming what I didn't want.

One day while praying, the Holy Spirit gently corrected me:

"You're speaking against your own future."

That moment hit me hard and opened my eyes. I was emotionally reinforcing negative expectations and teaching my nervous system to anticipate disappointment. I wasn't preparing my heart to receive, I was preparing it to retreat.

Do you remember the **Scar Experiment** from Chapter Three, The Beautiful You? The words we speak to ourselves shape how we show up. It's not just mindset, it's heart-set. And it matters.

So, I made a bold decision:

I flipped the script.

I started speaking declarations of faith, joy, and fulfillment as if they had already come to pass. I attached excitement to them. I envisioned my husband. I saw myself thriving in a God-ordained relationship. And most importantly, I believed.

Now, it's your turn.

Let's write and speak declarations that align your heart with your future.

Declarations that declare you are no longer the woman who waits in fear, you are the woman who rises in faith.

> *MENTAL BARRIERS WERE CREATED THROUGH WORDS AND REPETITION. THEY CAN BE DISMANTLED THROUGH NEW WORDS AND REPETITION.*
> MYLES MUNROE

Before we write our soulmate declarations.

Let's take a quick awareness check-up and clear the heart space of any hidden love blockers.

Before we speak life over our future, we need to be honest about what we've already been saying, especially the negative declarations we may have repeated out of frustration, fear, or disappointment.

I know this step personally. I had to recognize and rewrite the silent (and sometimes loud!) narratives that were keeping me stuck. We can't attract a healthy, loving relationship while unknowingly declaring its opposite.

This moment is about identifying those limiting beliefs and replacing them with truth-filled, faith-fueled declarations.

Take a few moments to reflect.

What negative declarations or self-talk have you been repeating, either out loud or in your thoughts?

Below is a sample chart to help spark awareness. After reviewing it, you'll create your own list using the blank chart on the next page.

Example: Awareness Table: Transforming Your Thought Life

Negative Thought	Positive Opposite Thought / Truth
"There are no good men out there."	*"There ARE good men, and God is leading me to one."*
"I'm not worthy of love."	*"I am deeply loved, worthy, and valued."*
"I'll always attract the wrong kind of man."	*"I attract emotionally healthy, godly men."*
"I'm too old / too late for love."	*"God's timing is perfect, my best love story is still unfolding."*
"I need to be perfect to be loved."	*"I am loved and lovable exactly as I am."*
"If I set boundaries, I'll scare men away."	*"Boundaries protect me and attract the right man."*
"I have to settle or I'll be alone."	*"I will not settle. I attract the man of my dreams."*
"All men will hurt or disappoint me."	*"Not all men are bad. I will attract and (trust God) to bring me a man who values, honors, and cherishes me."*
"If I show my true self, I'll be rejected."	*"The right man will love and celebrate the real me."*

Write down your negative and positive declarations that
came to mind below. You'll use this as a guide for the
declaration.

Negative Thought	Positive Opposite Thought / Truth

> ***DEATH AND LIFE ARE IN THE POWER OF THE TONGUE.***
> PROVERBS 18:21A KJV

Great job! Isn't this fun? We're re-writing your love story!

Remember, your inner dialogue, what you believe and expect, directly shapes how you show up in love and how others respond to you.

This is why your declarations matter. They aren't just affirmations, they are a spiritual reset, a new frequency. It's a mindset shift that says, *"I'm no longer walking in rejection, fear, or past programming. I'm walking in power, God's purpose, and the mindset of a queen."*

- Your words are shaping your world.
- Your declarations are either attracting or repelling the love you desire.
- The emotion behind your words is what activates your brain's response.

If you speak what you don't want with emotion, you're reinforcing fear. But when you speak what you do want with faith and excitement, you're retraining your mind and aligning your life with love's purpose.

Let's begin crafting your Soulmate Declarations, one of the most powerful tools in manifesting the love you're destined for.

You've already done deep heart work in this book. You've identified and exposed negative thought patterns that once shaped your beliefs about yourself, men, and relationships. By bringing those thoughts into the light and rewriting them with positive truths, you've already begun shifting your inner world.

Now, we take it a step further: you will intentionally create and speak powerful love declarations, positive, faith-filled statements that align your heart, your words, and your energy with what you truly desire.

This is where you go from awareness to attraction. You're going to write clear, intentional declarations about the man you are calling in, based on the values you defined, the truths you've embraced, and the love story you are ready to receive.

Your words are seeds. Speak them boldly. Expect them to take root and bear good fruit.

You are about to put pen to paper and begin co-creating the relationship your heart is prepared for.

I've included a sample of my personal soulmate declarations, words I spoke every day, like taking daily vitamins.

Here's a personal example from my own journey (yours will be unique!):

"My husband loves me like no one has ever loved me. He is the man of my dreams, my life partner. He loves to travel and change the world with me! He is a mighty man of God, filled with the Holy Spirit, with utmost integrity and honesty, completely trustworthy in every way. He has worked through any issues (sexual or otherwise) and has been completely delivered for years prior to meeting me".

My husband is funny, energetic, kindhearted, generous, and brilliantly smart. He knows how to adjust my back with chiropractic adjustments. We make each other laugh. He is open-minded and coachable. He has a wonderful business mind, and we are equally yoked spiritually! He loves and celebrates the gifts within me, as I do the same for him. He's my #1 supporter. His family loves and accepts me. My family and friends love him. We are the perfect match. We have an amazing life traveling the world together, changing people's lives with our message.

Did I get everything on this list, and more? YESSS! Did I have the skills (everything listed in this book) to nurture and grow our relationship when I met him? YESSS!

God is preparing the man who deserves you. You deserve the best, and he deserves the best version of you. Remember, it's worth the work and the wait!

Now it's time to create your world! On the next page, you'll find space to journal your declarations.

> *THE ONLY WAY TO ATTRACT WHAT YOU DESERVE IS TO BELIEVE YOU DESERVE IT AND LIVE LIKE YOU DO*
>
> UNKNOWN

Write your declarations here.

_____

_____

_____

_____

_____

_____

_____

_____

_____

_____

_____

_____

_____

_____

_____

_____

_____

_____

_____

_____

_____

_____

_____

_____

_____

_____

_____

_____

_____

_____

_____

Step 3: Create Your Soulmate Vision

When you see it, you believe it. When you believe it, you begin to receive it.

The final step is to bring your soulmate vision to life visually.

You can create a Vision Board or a Vision Book, a special space where you gather images, words, and symbols that represent the relationship you are calling in and the life you desire to build together.

Here's how:

- Cut out photos of couples that reflect love, connection, fun, and respect.
- Add quotes, scriptures, or declarations that anchor your heart in truth.
- Include images that symbolize peace, joy, shared hobbies, adventure, spiritual unity, and family life.
- Use colors, textures, and designs that evoke warmth and feel like home to your heart.
- Feel free to draw or write personal words or prayers onto your vision board or book.

This is not about just wishing, it's about creating a visual representation of the life and love you are aligning with.

Now it's time to create your dream book or board! We would love to see pictures of your vision board on the FB Solo to Soulmate Sisterhood page!

I still have my vision book that I created thirteen years ago. Every so often, I update it with new images and words. It has been my source of inspiration and a consistent reminder of where I was, how far I've come, and where I'm still headed.

Your vision board or book will help do the same for you. I'm so excited for you!

L7 MANIFESTO

Learn . . . to receive from others.

Light . . . up the world with your smile.

Love . . . yourself.

Laugh . . . to heal your soul.

Leap . . . out of your fears.

Let . . . him be your superhero.

Launch . . . into your destiny now!

Joanna Hairabedian

> *SEE, I AM DOING A NEW THING! NOW IT SPRINGS UP; DO YOU NOT PERCEIVE IT? I AM MAKING A WAY IN THE WILDERNESS AND STREAMS IN THE WASTELAND.*
> ISAIAH 43:19 NIV

CLOSING THOUGHTS

Excellent job!! You've done powerful heart work through these chapters! You've faced hard truths, rewritten old mindsets, and begun crafting a vision for a love story that honors the radiant, wise woman you are becoming.

I am SO PROUD of you! You are now in a stronger, more aligned mindset to attract Mr. Right and experience the kind of romance and love your heart truly desires. You are armed, equipped, and empowered to make life-giving changes that will bring new relationship results and beautiful blessings into your journey.

Today, I speak life, love, and healing over you! May every chapter you've completed open new doors of hope and joy. I'll leave you with my personal motto: The BEST is yet to come for you.

And remember this: You are not the same woman who started this book!

You are wiser. You are more self-aware. You are more whole. You have increased emotional intelligence and new relationship skills. You are now fully aligned with the kind of love God desires to bring into your life.

So, keep walking forward, with expectancy, faith, and joy. Speak life. Hold your vision close. Trust God's perfect timing and divine orchestration.

You are rewriting your love story!

And most of all, enjoy this season. Love is not a destination, it is a beautiful journey of becoming. And you, Queen, are already on the path.

If your heart is stirred to go even deeper, to continue this transformational journey with personal support and guidance... I invite you to explore my coaching program @ **FromSolotoSoulmate.com**

Together, we'll take this work to the next level, helping you fully step into your worth, heal at the deepest levels, and align with the kind of love story your heart is destined for.

You don't have to walk this path alone. If you're ready, I'm here to walk it with you. I look forward to celebrating your love story, one that will glorify God, honor your worth, and bless your future in ways you can't yet imagine.

With love and great expectation,

Joanna Hairabedian

EPILOGUE

A WORD FROM JOANNA'S HUSBAND, DR. DAVID

J oanna is also writing a book for men, and I jokingly suggested the title should be *7,000 Mistakes Men Make That Repel Good Women.*

All kidding aside, I don't think women always realize that men are searching for their perfect match too, just like women are. Instead of acknowledging their desire for a life partner, many men get distracted by work, career goals, sports, or other pursuits.

I was one of those men, disconnected from my deeper needs, substituting my drive for success for real connection. Until I met Joanna.

As a Type A personality who always seems to have an answer, I was stunned one day when Joanna asked me a simple question: *"What do you like to do for fun?"*

I was speechless. I didn't have an answer. No one had ever asked me that before. And in that moment, it hit me, I wasn't truly living. I was just going through the motions alone.

Joanna awakened something in me. She drew out parts of me I didn't know, that have learned how to laugh, have fun, and truly enjoy life.

This is my first marriage, and after being single for a long time, I could never have imagined how rich and fulfilling our marriage would be. I know my heart is safe in Joanna's hands, just as hers is safe in mine.

Ultimately, I had been searching for my queen, someone I could build with, dream with, and change the world alongside. And now, I've found her. And together, that's exactly what we're doing.

There's something powerful about finding true partnership, it accelerates everything. That's exactly what marriage to Joanna has been for me.

As King Solomon said:

"Two are better than one, because they have a good return for their labor. If either of them falls down, one can help the other up." Ecclesiastes 4:9–10 (NIV)

> ***HE WHO FINDS A WIFE FINDS A GOOD THING AND***
> ***OBTAINS FAVOR FROM THE LORD.***
> PROVERBS 18:22 NKJV

I love that Joanna has become the missing wind beneath my wings, and I am hers. She is my perfect puzzle piece match, and we truly do everything together. She lives out every bit of what she teaches others, with authenticity and grace.

I love you, Joanna.

The best is yet to come!

Dr. David Hairabedian

ABOUT THE AUTHOR

Joanna Hairabedian, Relationship Coach is best known as **The Soulmate Strategist™** and is the creator of the **Solo to Soulmate Method™**.

It's a transformational, faith-based coaching program that helps single women heal from heartbreak, build emotional resilience, and attract aligned, lasting love.

She's also the author of *"7 Mistakes Women Make That Repel Good Men and How to Reverse Them."*

A three-time national pageant winner, including **Ms. America 2019–21,** Joanna empowers women to shine from within by uncovering what she calls their **"Diamond Within®"**, the unique brilliance God placed inside each woman. As a composer, vocal artist, and TV producer, Joanna has learned how to utilize her gifts to help transform people's lives.

Through her **Women of Royalty™** conferences and programs, Joanna helps women step into their royal identity and rewrite their love stories with confidence and clarity.

Joanna and her wonderful husband, Dr. David Hairabedian found their happily ever after and married in 2014. They have a beautiful marriage and are co-founders of an online spiritual equipping platform called **VirtualChurchMedia.com**.

Together they are sought-after international speakers, ministers and have impacted millions of lives around the world.

Download the mobile app for **VirtualChurchMedia.com** that features all kinds of wonderful and complimentary spiritual equipping tools, books, podcasts, TV broadcasts and more.

VCM Mobile App

Appendix A

Spiritual Healing Prayers

> ## HE HEALS THE BROKENHEARTED AND HEALS UP
>
> ## THEIR WOUNDS.
>
> PSALM 147;3 NKJV

There are moments in life when words fall short, but prayer never does.

Whether you're navigating emotional wounds, past heartbreaks, or simply seeking deeper intimacy with God, prayer is a powerful tool that invites divine healing into your life. God is the Author of healing, and His presence brings peace, restoration, and transformation.

Included in this appendix is prayer for breakthrough. May these words become a lifeline when your heart needs strength, a compass when you feel lost, and a bridge between your past and your promise.

If you need additional spiritual resources, our Virtual Church Media mobile app has all kinds of complimentary (paid for by our donors) books, teachings, podcasts, etc. on various topics from hearing God's voice to breaking deferred hope to relationship.

You can download it at www.VirtualChurchMedia.com

As you pray, remember: You're not alone, and mountains still move through prayer. God loves you deeply, even when you don't feel it.

Prayer...

Heavenly Father, your precious daughter and I come before the throne of heaven right now. We stand before Your amazing grace and ask forgiveness for our sins, mistakes, poor choices, and any areas of compromise. We thank you, Heavenly Father, that Your Beloved Son died on the cross so that we can be cleansed in our souls of everything and healed in our bodies.

The Word says that you heal the brokenhearted and bind up our wounds. By the power of the Holy Spirit, in the name of your Precious Son, I release healing and strength in the heart, mind, body, soul, and spirit for Your daughter who is reading this!

I pray over YOU, daughter of the King of heaven, for the mighty hand of God to overshadow every situation in your life right now. I pray for the baptism of His love to fill your soul and heart like never before. I commission the angels of God to move on behalf of you and your family in Jesus' name. Psalm 91 says that He will command his angels to guard you! I pray for every crooked path in your life to be straightened out.

I pray for the old mirror of the way you see yourself to be replaced with Heaven's mirror. From this point forward, I pray that you will see yourself through the loving eyes of your heavenly Father. I break off the spirit of trauma and infirmity in your life and release the light, healing, and love of God to fill you now in Jesus' name.

Every lying spirit and thing that torments or haunts you at night is broken off. My prayer is for peace to overcome that torment. I pray that any toxic people in your life will be divinely removed and blessed somewhere else and replaced with new people God has assigned to help you. I commission the Angels of God to do a spiritual house cleaning. Psalm 91 says that you will rest in the Shadow of the Almighty and under His wings you'll find refuge.

Daughter of the King of Heaven, I bless you today with supernatural peace (shalom), with joy, with prosperity, with love, with healing, with wholeness, with health and a new mirror to see yourself as God sees you. I bless your coming in and going out. In Jesus' name and by the power of the Holy Spirit I pray these things. AMEN.

A Special Invitation...

> AND THE PRAYER OF FAITH SHALL SAVE THE SICK, AND THE LORD SHALL RAISE HIM UP; AND IF HE HAS COMMITTED SINS, THEY SHALL BE FORGIVEN HIM. CONFESS YOUR FAULTS ONE TO ANOTHER, AND PRAY ONE FOR ANOTHER, THAT YE MAY BE HEALED. THE EFFECTUAL FERVENT PRAYER OF A RIGHTEOUS MAN AVAILETH MUCH.
>
> JAMES 5:15-17 KJV

Are you aware of the special invitation to a heavenly banquet just for you? Read on...

Did you know that everyone has a special invitation to a beautiful banquet in heaven? However, just like any gala, we have to RSVP for this incredible event. Would you like to RSVP? Do you need a new identity? You can be born again as a new person in Christ.

Here's how you do it: Invite Jesus into your heart and ask Him for a personal relationship. He's been waiting for you. Ask Him to forgive all your sins and fill you with His Holy Spirit.

No matter what you've done or what's been done to you, those things are washed away because of the precious Blood of Jesus that He shed on the cross. He was crucified on a cross for your sins so that you can be born again. When you acknowledge Jesus as your Lord and Savior, your life will change for eternity, and you can attend the beautiful banquet in heaven. He wants you to get to know Him and be in a relationship with Him.

Prayer to Accept the Invitation to Heaven

Jesus, I invite you into my heart for a personal relationship with me today. I confess all my mistakes and sins to you and ask for forgiveness. Change my heart, change my mindset, and baptize me in Your Holy Spirit. I choose to serve You. Fill my heart with a love, healing, and passion I've never known. In Your name, I pray. AMEN

Congratulations! Heaven is rejoicing right now for you!

Prayer for Baptism with the Holy Spirit and Fire
With a short teaching

The Baptism of the Holy Spirit is a divine empowerment from God. It's not just for speaking in tongues, though that may be one of the gifts, but it's about receiving boldness, spiritual authority, deeper intimacy with the Lord, and the fire to walk in your Kingdom calling. As John the Baptist said in Matthew 3:11, "He will baptize you with the Holy Spirit and fire." This fire purifies, ignites passion, and burns away anything that no longer serves God's purpose in your life.

This is not about striving, it's about receiving. You don't earn this gift; you simply position yourself in hunger and humility, saying, "Lord, I want more of You." You may experience a powerful sense of His presence, deep peace, holy fire, tears, joy, a new language (tongues), or simply stillness. However it manifests, trust that God knows how to give good gifts to His children (Luke 11:13).

Now, let's pray...

Heavenly Father, you promised that we could be baptized with the Holy Spirit and with fire. Today, I boldly come before You, hungry and expectant. I don't want anything less than what You've designed for my life. I want to walk in power, love, and full alignment with Heaven.

I ask now, fill me with Your Holy Spirit and fire. Burn away anything in me that would hinder my walk with Jesus or block my ability to love and serve others with purity and strength. Empower me to be bold, sensitive to Your voice, and effective in my calling.

I receive it now, by faith. Now pause. Sit in His presence. Let His Spirit minister to your heart. Listen for His whispers. Feel His fire cleansing and filling you. He is faithful to give what He promises.

If you need spiritual equipping, tools, teaching, etc. then please download this mobile app for **VirtualChurchMedia.com**. This app offers great learning and life equipping resources, books, etc. as a gift to you. It is sponsored by the donors and others who want to pay it forward.

VCM Mobile App

Virtual Church Media also features podcasts, TV broadcasts, healing music, and a one-year Bible study. Learning the Bible is crucial because it serves as an amazing life guide.

Prayer for Deliverance and Deferred Hope

Deferred Hope: A Short Teaching & Deliverance Prayer
Based on Proverbs 13:12 (NKJV) – "Hope deferred makes the heart sick, but a desire fulfilled is a tree of life."

Deferred hope isn't just disappointment, it's the weight of lingering sadness, delay, and disillusionment that settles deep in the soul. It can make us spiritually weary, emotionally numb, or even begin to doubt God's promises over our lives. The danger of deferred hope is that it slowly robs you of vision, expectation, and joy. Left unchecked, it becomes a spiritual stronghold that hinders faith, blocks intimacy, and clouds your ability to receive love.

But God is not a God of delay, He is a God of perfect timing and restoration. When hope has been deferred, it doesn't mean it's been denied. It simply means the enemy tried to wear you out while you waited. Today, we break that lie. We reclaim the promises and we release healing to your hope.

You're not disqualified, delayed, or forgotten. You're being set up for a tree-of-life moment.

Let's pray…

Deferred Hope Deliverance Prayer

Lord, I recognize my need for deliverance from deferred hope. I humbly come before You and ask in the Name of Jesus to set me free from every stronghold of disappointment, delay, and despair. I renounce the enemy's lies, spiritual resistance, and negative words spoken over my life, knowingly or unknowingly.

Deferred hope, I name you and break your hold over my life right now in Jesus' Name. I command you to depart and never return. In your place, I release the promise of a desire fulfilled, which Scripture says is like a tree of life (Proverbs 13:12 *NKJV*).

I release the joy of Heaven to fill my heart now and choose today to believe God's promises again. I declare God, that no good thing will You withhold from those who walk uprightly. I believe You are restoring what has been lost or delayed. Father, show me Your faithfulness in a tangible way this week so that my hope may be anchored in truth, not circumstances. The blood of Jesus covers me. I receive a fresh injection of divine light and hope to rise up in me. Strength returns. Joy overflows. From this moment forward, I declare full restoration over my soul. I release the mind of Christ to guide and guard my mind and heart now in Jesus' Name, Amen.

Prayer for Holy Spirit Baptism & Empowerment

"If you then, being evil, know how to give good gifts to your children, how much more will your Heavenly Father give the Holy Spirit to those who ask Him!" – Luke 11:13 (NKJV)

The Baptism of the Holy Spirit is a divine gift of empowerment, designed to fill you with boldness, love, spiritual authority, and an intimate connection with God. It's not just for preachers, missionaries, or "extra spiritual" people, it's for you.

When you receive the Holy Spirit baptism, it's like Heaven breathes on you afresh. You may receive a prayer language (tongues), a spiritual gift that allows you to pray God's perfect will, edify yourself, and access supernatural peace. This prayer language doesn't make you "better" than anyone else—it simply makes you more equipped, more aligned, and more sensitive to God's presence.

If you've ever felt powerless, dry, or spiritually stuck, this is the refreshing you've been longing for.

Let's pray the Holy Spirit Baptism Prayer.

Heavenly Father, I thank You for the precious gifts You have freely given to Your children. Your Word in Luke 11:13 *(NKJV)* promises that if earthly parents know how to give good gifts, how much more will You give the Holy Spirit to those who ask.

So today, by faith, I ask You for the baptism of the Holy Spirit, with fire, love, and power, in Jesus' Mighty Name. I repent of anything I've believed, said, or partnered with that has resisted this gift. Wash me clean and align me with truth. I also ask for my personal prayer language, that I may speak mysteries to You in private and release Your power in public.

I fully expect to receive this now. Fill me, Holy Spirit. Flow through me. Set my heart ablaze with love, courage, and intimacy with You. In Jesus' Name, Amen.

Now Take Time to Receive

Find a quiet space. If you feel comfortable, lift your hands like a child reaching for their Father. You may begin to sense a bubbling sensation or a new language rising from deep within you, this is often how tongues begin. Don't overthink it. Just surrender and let it flow.

It may come in a whisper, a song, or a syllable. Trust God. The Holy Spirit is gentle and will meet you in your faith. Just as you once gave your voice to fear, anger, or the enemy, now give it to God.

When you allow the Holy Spirit to move through your words, your atmosphere will shift, your heart will heal, and your spirit will soar. This is your moment. Let Heaven fill you.

If you need spiritual equipment, tools, teaching, etc. then please download this mobile app for **VirtualChurchMedia.com**.

VCM Mobile App

This app offers great learning and life equipping resources, books, etc. as a gift to you. It is sponsored by the donors and others who want to pay it forward.

VirtualChurchMedia.com also features podcasts, TV broadcasts, healing music, and a one-year Bible study. Learning the Bible is crucial because it serves as an amazing life guide.

God bless you and your family!

Appendix 1B & 2B - Resources

BIOHACK YOUR BODY AND HEALTH

> *IF YOU WANT TO FIND THE SECRETS OF THE UNIVERSE*
> *THINK IN TERMS OF ENERGY, FREQUENCY AND VIBRATION.*
> NIKOLA TESLA

Need some changes in your health for the better?

For the full document…go to this link: solotosoulmate.com

We are currently bombarded with more toxic exposure from water, food, air, and electronic smog than ever before. My husband David and I are also in ministry, and we are flooded with calls every week from people who need prayer for themselves, family members who are very sick, have emotional anxiety or dying. We've never seen anything like this.

I'm continuously asked what I do for my health and wellness, so I created this resources page. Our bodies need as much assistance as possible in this current toxic environment. As usual, I always encourage everyone to take responsibility and do their own research. Give yourself permission to change your mind, given new information.

This information is intended for educational and research purposes, because when women ask me, *"What did you use to feel whole and healthy again?"* I don't just want to answer… I want to empower. I think you'll find this information very interesting.

These are the very tools I personally used during my healing journey, tools that helped me feel stronger, clearer, more radiant, and most importantly, helped me **reclaim my life**. While results may vary, what matters most is that you give yourself permission to explore and discover what resonates with *you*.

First...the necessary disclaimer *(disclosure also at front of my book, From Solo to Soulmate).*

Disclaimer

The author and publisher is not a medical or licensed doctor or therapist. The content provided in this book is intended for educational purposes and results may vary. Each person is responsible for the choices they make and results they may experience. These products and resources have not been evaluated by the FDA and are not intended to treat, cure or diagnose any diseases or issues. They are not intended to substitute for medical advice, diagnosis or treatment. Consult your healthcare provider about any concerns, medical issues, mental health conditions, taking or starting any new supplement, health regime or alternative therapies, etc. Supplements are not medicine or drugs.

Some of the links and resources mentioned in this section may be affiliate links. If you choose to purchase through these links, I may receive a referral commission at no additional cost to you. I only recommend products and technologies that I personally use, trust, and believe can genuinely support the wellness journey. Your support helps me continue providing valuable content to serve and empower women like you!

One of the core themes throughout *From Solo To Soulmate* has been *awakened awareness*, and the courage to change our minds, habits, and environments when new insight is revealed. We give ourselves permission to change our minds given new information. That same principle applies to how we care for our bodies and protect our peace.

Little keys unlock big doors. Big doors swing on small hinges. Good things done consistently add up to radiant health!

Ready to check out some exciting and fun technology alternatives?

Clean Skincare and Makeup That Works.
www.biohackmyskin.com

Your skin is the largest organ in the body and what you put on directly absorbs into your system. I've searched high and low for skincare and make-up that **actually** isn't formulated with toxic chemicals and provides actual results!

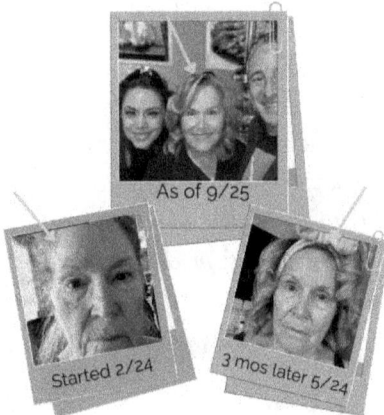

As of 9/25

Started 2/24

3 mos later 5/24

Well, my prayers were answered with this skincare line!

The woman in this picture is my 80-yr old friend, Dr. Susan D. The results she got were using the "Ritual Signature Facial". Check out the website for the info.

People who haven't seen me for a long period of time will often make comments like, *"What are you using on your skin? You never seem to age."*

As we age, we all need help counteracting the aging process. Feeling beautiful and cared for in your own skin is a key part of radiating confidence and attracting the right kind of attention. Have fun exploring the site. **www.biohackmyskin.com**

PEMF Frequency Therapy for the body
www.biohackyourself.us

Are you familiar with ChatGPT or Perplexity? If not, I highly recommend using it. Then type in the prompt and ask what the benefits of PEMF frequency are. What will come up will astound you.

Ever heard of PEMA (Pulsed Electro Magnetic Activation) frequency? Check that out as well.

Molecular activation is a key. Active molecules mean pure life energy, recharging your batteries. Everything is made up of molecules. Water, stone, wood, bone, hair, nails, and cells. Literally everything, even our blood, is made up of molecules.

My favorite PEMF device for molecular activation is the KLOUD mat by CENTROPIX. It has played a huge role in helping me take back my health.

Dr. Kafka, the brilliant scientist behind this amazing technology of CENTROPIX, was featured on the cover with an 8-page spread in the prestigious *Top Doctor Magazine*. Dr. Kafka has taken PEMF (Pulsed Electro Magnetic Frequency) to the next level with PEMA (Pulsed Electro Magnetic Activation).

In addition, CENTROPIX was featured in an awesome documentary called *Biohack Yourself*, an Amazon Prime docu-series. It showcases innovative technologies to combat the effects of aging, enhanced vitality, longevity, improved sleep, increased relaxation and taking back your health.

For a deeper dive into this technology, you can research it on the website that breaks it all down. www.biohackyourself.us

Vibing to the Earth's Frequencywww.frequencybiohack.com

My go-to frequency *wearable* is called the BUBBLE by CENTROPIX. Shaped like its name, this sleek device hangs comfortably around your neck and allows you to immerse your body in healthy frequencies.

I can tune my BUBBLE to the Earth's natural Schumann Resonance or choose any Solfeggio frequency between 1 Hz and 1000 Hz. It helps keep my biofield aligned, balanced, and energetically protected. Solfeggio frequency 528 is known as the healing frequency of love. Check it out on ChatGPT or Perplexity.

For example, if you've ever felt foggy, fatigued, felt heat in your head or hand from holding the phone or "off" without explanation, this resource may open your eyes to an invisible culprit and what you can do to protect your peace. Appendix 2B has an explanation and definition of "toxic ticks" from various sources.

One of my naturopathic doctors explained it like this, he said, *"It's all about exposure to E-Smog micro toxic ticks. Think of your cells as cups. Each time you are exposed to a micro toxic tick there's a little more that goes into your cup."* It's an accumulative effect and when your cup is full, that's when health issues or symptoms can manifest."

In Appendix 2B, you can also learn about the importance of the earth's magnetic frequencies called the Schumann resonances and Solfeggio therapeutic frequencies. For example, if you type into ChatGPT or Perplexity about the benefits of one of the Solfeggio frequencies of 528 Htz frequency (known as the frequency of love), you'll be amazed!

Learn more at **www.frequencybiohack.com**.

Beginners Detox Regime www.biohackerdetox.com

What I love about Vital Health is the quality of ingredients, the very reasonable price points and the integrity of this company. They own all their own labs and have an incredible board of certified MD's and Naturopathic Doctors with varying backgrounds in health.

VitalHealth offers cutting-edge wellness products focused on cellular energy, gut health, and optimal body function. I love their **starter basic detox package** that supports kidney, liver, gut, helps reduce sugar cravings and supports metabolism.

For nourishment of my body and collagen building, my personal regime also includes their sublingual Glutathione Plus, V-Daily (a blend of non-synthetic vitamins, minerals, amino acids, probiotics, and superfoods to support energy, digestion, and whole-body wellness), Vitalage Collagen (tissue-supporting nutrients to restore skin elasticity, strengthen joints, supports microbiome health and internal radiance.)

Their formulas leverage advanced bioactive ingredients to support vitality, detoxing, mental clarity, and overall well-being. When your body is fueled well, you show up in the world with more energy, confidence, and magnetism.

Concluding Thoughts. Honoring Your Temple

I hope these tips and tools have inspired you and offered something meaningful for your wellness journey. Our bodies are miraculous vessels, designed by God to heal, radiate, and thrive. That's why biohacking isn't just a trend; it's a sacred invitation to realign with how you were divinely designed to live: whole, vibrant, and radiant from the inside out.

Whether it's using frequency-based therapies to restore balance, choosing skincare that heals instead of harms, or gently detoxifying what no longer serves you, every intentional step makes a difference.